TWENTIETH CENTURY VIEWS

The aim of this series is to present the best in contemporary critical opinion on major authors, providing a twentieth century perspective on their changing status in an era of profound revaluation.

Maynard Mack, *Series Editor*
Yale University

A U D E N

A COLLECTION OF CRITICAL ESSAYS

Edited by

Monroe K. Spears

Prentice-Hall, Inc., *Englewood Cliffs, N. J.*

Acknowledgment is gratefully made to Random House, Inc. and Faber & Faber, Ltd. for quotation from *The Collected Poetry of W. H. Auden* (the English edition is entitled *Collected Shorter Poems*): "Petition" (*Poems*), copyright 1934 and renewed 1961 by W. H. Auden; "Dover 1937" and "The hourglass whispers to the lion's roar" (also entitled "Our Bias") (*Another Time*), copyright 1940 by W. H. Auden; "Song" ("Look, stranger, on this island now") (*On This Island*), copyright 1937 by W. H. Auden; Sonnet I from "In Time of War" (*The Collected Poetry of W. H. Auden*), copyright 1945 by W. H. Auden, and the three lines from "The Shield of Achilles," by W. H. Auden, which appear on the cover and jacket.

Current printing (last digit):
11 10 9 8 7 6 5 4

ENGLEWOOD CLIFFS, N.J.

LIBRARY OF CONGRESS CATALOG CARD NO.: 64-19682

Printed in the United States of America—C

P 05070
C 05071

Table of Contents

Introduction

by Monroe K. Spears

I

Most good criticism of Auden is recent, for during the greater part of his thirty-five years of fame as poet, Auden has been peculiarly unfortunate in the treatment accorded him by reviewers and critics. At the beginning of his career he was greeted by excesses of praise, on grounds largely irrelevant to the true nature of his poetry: he was hailed as the leader of a "group" with a political program, as a poetic messiah who would lead the way out of the Waste Land. When politically oriented critics saw that he was not what they had wanted him to be, the reaction was bitter, and it became bitterer still when he emigrated to the United States and began writing religious poetry. Resentment of Auden as a Lost Leader was an obvious motive, though rarely an ostensible one, in much criticism of the later Thirties and the Forties, and it still survives.

On the other hand, aesthetically oriented critics were generally made suspicious by Auden's popularity and the outcry about his politics, as well as by his facility and occasional unevenness. Though some critics of this type have written well about Auden, he has never been one of their central concerns or enthusiasms. The most influential of all hostile criticism of Auden was that of F. R. Leavis and his followers, whose criteria appeared to be aesthetic but were, it seems clear in retrospect, basically moral and social. Though Leavis allowed Auden promise and published occasional reviews by him in *Scrutiny* from 1932 to 1935, Auden soon became the whipping boy for the group's profound antipathy to Oxford, Bloomsbury, and the academic and literary Establishments which had, they thought, made Auden fashionable. The recognition of Auden's promise was accompanied by forebodings for the future: as early as 1933 Leavis pronounced that *The Orators* was an ominous falling off from the *Poems* of 1930. Soon Auden was "placed" as immature, "arrested at the stage of undergraduate 'brilliance.' " Leavis established this view so early in Auden's career that one wonders at the assurance with which he dismissed Auden's future as hopeless and damned him for good; one suspects that the judgment, being an integral part of *Scrutiny* orthodoxy, was an article of faith and not subject to change. As Leavis summed it up in the "Epilogue" to the second edition of *New Bearings in English Poetry,*[1] speaking of "Paid on Both Sides" (1930): "It seems to me that Auden has hardly come nearer to essential maturity since, though he made a rapid advance in sophistication." Auden's arrested development is then considered as a case history, a cautionary tale showing the effects of "uncritical acclamation," the "failure of the function of criticism," the "disintegration of the educated reading public," and the domination of the literary world instead by a coterie and the values of fashion and social class. In the "Retrospect" appended to the recent reprint of *Scrutiny,* Leavis reveals the extent to which Auden became a mythical figure, a kind of culture villain, or victim, for the group. He asserts that *Scrutiny's* major negative service "was to deal firmly with the 'Poetical Renascence,' the coterie movement that opened triumphantly in the early 'thirties." *Scrutiny* pointed out "that Auden, with his modish, glib, and sophisticated immaturity couldn't go on being credited with promise if, gainsaying the ominous characteristics, he didn't soon begin to prove himself capable of developing." But he didn't develop, and in spite of Keynes, Bloomsbury, the *New Statesman,* and the Public School Communists and fellow travelers, *Scrutiny* repeatedly affirmed and enforced the verdict. Leavis concludes with some complacency:

> Thirty years after we put the case against Auden it passes as a commonplace. True, there is a suggestion that he has "gone off," and that it is the late Auden who compels the current adverse criticism. But if the criticism is admitted, then the Auden of no phase can be saved. And in fact that has been implicitly granted. Quietly, by tacit consent, his spell of glory has lapsed. . . .[2]

Scrutiny was, of course, negative toward almost all contemporary poetry, with the partial exceptions of Yeats, Eliot, and Ronald Bottrall, but the case against Auden was pressed with special vigor, and with motives at least in part transparently extraliterary. His defects could be

[1] F. R. Leavis, *New Bearings in English Poetry* (New York: George W. Stewart, Publisher, Inc., 1950), p. 227.

[2] *Scrutiny,* XX, 16 (Cambridge: Cambridge University Press, 1963). Since this last volume of the reprint edition contains a very full index, I do not give references to the various considerations of Auden, by Leavis and others, that were published from time to time throughout the history of the journal.

dealt with more in sorrow than in anger, as not so much his own fault as the result of the lack of critical standards and an educated public: an object lesson in the effect of Oxford frivolity and coterie standards. The verdict was spelled out by many of Leavis's followers. In 1945 R. G. Lienhardt, reviewing *For the Time Being* in *Scrutiny,* called his review "Auden's Inverted Development." His severity exceeds even Leavis's: Auden's "only claim to importance rests on effects produced almost casually in his early work," and he is dismissed finally with the contemptuous observation that he has "the mental equipment only of a minor poet." The *Scrutiny* campaign exerted a powerful and continuing influence: Richard Hoggart, writing the first full-scale book on Auden in 1951, acknowledged that his view of Auden's career had been influenced by Lienhardt's review,[3] and R. G. Cox, in the chapter on Auden in the *Pelican Guide to English Literature,*[4] plainly still reflects it.

Two American critics who do not quite fit into either of the preceding categories (though both have more political orientation than appears on the surface) have also done profound damage to Auden's reputation. Randall Jarrell, in two brilliant essays of 1941 and 1945,[5] "unmasked" Auden's "ideologies" as no more than a series of rationalizations of his own psychological peculiarities, and analyzed the texture of his later verse as a constant degeneration from the earliest. The result was a striking picture of intellectual confusion and poetic decline, often highly perceptive in detail but, in my opinion, essentially false. With the passage of time, Jarrell's ideological argument has come to seem dated: now that more than twenty years have passed without significant change, it is no longer plausible to represent Auden as a man of rapidly shifting beliefs. As one looks back from the perspective of 1964, it is clear that the changes were confined to one brief period in the late Thirties, that they were all in the same direction, and that, once the fundamental commitment to Christianity had been fully made, the only changes were mere shifts of emphasis. Similarly, though Jarrell's detailed analysis of the rhetoric and attitudes of Auden's early verse remains

[3] Richard Hoggart, *Auden: An Introductory Essay* (London: Chatto and Windus, 1951), p. 232.

[4] See the Selected Bibliography at the end of this volume. When full information concerning a book or article mentioned in this introduction is not supplied in a footnote, it will be found in the Bibliography.

[5] Randall Jarrell, "Changes of Attitude and Rhetoric in Auden's Poetry," *The Southern Review,* VII (1941), 326-49; "Freud to Paul: The Stages of Auden's Ideology," *Partisan Review,* XII (1945), 437-57.

interesting and valuable, the conclusions he drew from it in 1941 no longer seem compelling.[6]

Joseph Warren Beach, in *The Making of the Auden Canon* (1957), made a detailed study of Auden's *Collected Poetry* (1945), considering Auden's revisions of his earlier work, his choice of which poems to preserve, and similar questions. Beach collected a tremendous mass of detailed information, bibliographical and textual, about Auden's poems, and examined it with care and thoroughness. But his study, for all its appearance of scholarly detachment, is very far from objective. Because Beach himself believes in a secular liberalism, he is profoundly suspicious of Auden's abandonment of that position and of his religious beliefs and attitudes. Thus, like the Leavisites, though from different motives, he tends to regard Auden's career as "inverted." His romantic conception of poetry makes him tend to regard all revision as a violation and desecration, while at the same time he reads the poetry primarily as a statement of ideas, so that he explains revisions almost entirely in terms of changes in Auden's ideas and beliefs. (Jarrell's articles probably helped to form his assumption that Auden's beliefs changed constantly, with no fixed center.) The picture that emerges is of Auden as a man uncertain of his own identity, irresponsibly and frivolously revising his work, and in the process disowning his past. Because of the amount of valuable material it contains and its appearance of scholarly authoritativeness, Beach's book has carried great weight, especially among academics.

The cumulative effect of the criticism I have described has been to create a widespread impression that Auden has been "proved" guilty of immaturity, frivolity, irresponsibility, and other vices, and is therefore not to be taken seriously. Minor critics speak of him with condescension and refer knowingly to his inverted development, his changes of ideology, and his mutilation of his earlier poetry when he deserted politics for religion. It is no wonder that Auden has always been skittish about critics and, though he himself has written a very large amount of criticism and is certainly one of the major critics of our time, has been unwilling until very recently to appear in this role by publishing a volume of selected criticism. There is a certain irony in the fact that this volume,[7] with its massive demonstration of Auden's maturity, seriousness and moral responsibility, has already done a good deal to dispel the myth that these qualities are lacking in the poetry.

[6] Had Mr. Jarrell been willing to grant permission, I would have included the essay of 1941, but he seems not to want either of his essays to be reprinted.

[7] *The Dyer's Hand and Other Essays* (New York: Random House, 1962).

I have described this kind of hostile criticism at some length because I do not include any of it in this collection. Instead of attempting to make the collection "representative," I have chosen only those essays that seem to me both illuminating and likely to retain some permanent value. These are isolated and individual pieces, not part of any critical trend (though the fact that most of them are recent suggests that there is a trend toward more satisfactory treatment of Auden). Since the early and brief enthusiasm of the Marxists, Auden has not been championed by any critical movement; the criticism that was required to explain and defend Eliot, for example, was largely irrelevant to Auden. For Auden is an old-fashioned or traditional poet in his conception of the poetic role, while at the same time highly modern in technique. He has no intention of restricting poetry to its quintessential function, its purest and most intense manifestations, as Eliot, for example, tends to do. Instead, he is a very impure poet indeed, copious, facile, and versatile. He writes to entertain and instruct, as well as to produce the more subtle and profound effects of poetry, and he deals often with contemporary ideas and topical events. He writes many different kinds of poetry, in highly varied styles and forms. Much of his verse trespasses on the ground of other literary forms that most poets now stay away from: thus many of his poems are compressed short stories, plays, or biographical or critical essays. He uses the traditional genres far more than most moderns—ode, sonnet, elegy, eclogue, song, epistle, oratorio, closet drama—and writes occasional poems on events public and private. He adopts the personae (including typical verse forms) of earlier poets from Langland to Blake, Burns, and Byron, and he does brilliant parodies and pastiches. He is an indefatigable teacher and gives his didactic impulse full reign.

At the same time he is one of the most inward and subjective of poets. Taken individually, his poems are often extremely obscure; they are therefore less suited than those of most modern poets to the kind of critical treatment that begins by considering the poem as an isolated, independent, and discrete entity. Taken together, however, his poems create a cosmos, a poetic universe with its repeated symbolic properties, from landscape to typical characters and recurrent situations. Modern critics can, of course, deal beautifully with the artist's construction of a private symbolic world (as in Kafka, early Eliot, late Yeats), but the mixture of this with the more external kinds of form discussed above, together with the outcry about Auden's politics, made them slow to see this aspect. Marxist critics soon found him too private, but "new" critics were already suspicious of him as too public; hence neither dealt with him satisfactorily. Similarly, the musical aspect of Auden's verse—the fact that he is the finest writer of songs, ballads, libretti, and other forms for music among the modern poets—has been recognized only slowly, because it is remote from the popular conception of Auden. Critics are no longer accustomed to dealing with such variety and copiousness.

In temperament and in quality of imagination as well as in interests, Auden is in some respects more like a scientist than like the typical modern poet. (William Empson is the only one who resembles him much in this regard.) His knowledge of biology and psychology is extensive and current, and he is widely read in anthropology, sociology, geology, and other related sciences. A certain tough-mindedness, a detachment, sometimes a remoteness, are manifest in his attitude; he often views human life from a great distance, concerning himself with the differences between man and the other animals and between man and the rest of nature, or with man in the vast perspective of geological or evolutionary time. Often his imagination tends to generalization, like that of a scientist: he frames hypotheses, as it were, and discerns patterns from specific instances. But this aspect of Auden must not be exaggerated: against this tendency to abstraction there is the vividly specific and concrete quality of his imagination (which leads Mr. Bayley even to call him Dickensian), and against the detachment and remoteness there are the compassion, tolerance, and sympathy for "ordinary" people and things that have grown more and more marked in his verse. Further, there is the concern with the supernatural, apparent not only in the religious aspect of the verse (which is present from the beginning) but also in the denial of the "magical" function of poetry and the later definitions of it as embodying "sacred awe."

II

So far, I have been concerned to suggest the extraliterary motives that have lain behind much of the hostile criticism of Auden and to explain why he has not been done justice by the dominant critical movements of our time. To come now to the present collection: most of these pieces were written in the last ten years, and they would seem to provide a basis for the hopeful generalization that criticism of Auden has been increasing in quality. There were, of course, some good pieces written earlier, and the first two essays in the collection are examples of these. (The essays are arranged in roughly chronological order.)

Christopher Isherwood's contribution to the "Auden Double Number" (1937) of *New Verse* is the earliest piece included. Isherwood, Auden's close friend from boyhood and his literary mentor for many years (as well as his collaborator on three plays), speaks with a unique authority about Auden's early verse. *Lions and Shadows,* his fictional autobiography, has a long chapter dealing with "Hugh Weston," his "caricature" of Auden, which is full of fascinating, if often dramatically heightened, material. The whole *New Verse* issue is still of interest, especially the pieces by the editor, Geoffrey Grigson, by Louis MacNeice, who also makes some useful comments in his *Modern Poetry,* and by Stephen Spender. Of Spender's numerous writings about Auden the present essay (1953) seems to me the most judicious and best balanced, though his autobiographical account in *World Within World* contains much valuable background. The other member of the so-called Auden "group" (who were not really a group at all), C. Day Lewis, did not write about Auden extensively until his recent autobiography, *The Buried Day;* by putting together the relevant passages from it and from the autobiographies of Isherwood and Spender, a vivid and amusing joint picture of Auden as a young man is produced.

The second early essay (1939) is that by Cleanth Brooks, who (in a book which, by the way, Auden reviewed favorably in *The Nation*) was one of the first to apply the "new criticism" fruitfully to Auden. Concerning himself primarily with the nature of Auden's imagery, Brooks concludes that his affinities are with the true central tradition of English poetry as it appears most plainly in the seventeenth-century "Metaphysical" poets. (The definition of this as the central tradition, like Leavis' very similar definition, is based on Eliot's suggestions, but Leavis would emphatically leave Auden out of it.) Such later critics as Bayley and Fraser, for example, take issue with Brooks's thesis, and argue that modern poetry, including Auden, is essentially Romantic. Since their arguments do not appear explicitly in the excerpts from their books included in this volume, there is no need to discuss them here. I will, however, briefly indicate two pragmatic objections. In the first place, the typical modern poets—Pound, Eliot, Auden—have not thought of themselves as Romantics; they thought they were revolting against late Romanticism, and to argue that they were self-deceived tends to discredit them. Further, no matter how innocuously "Romantic" is defined, the popular connotation of ineffectual dreaminess, retreat from reality into wishful thinking, lingers on, and the argument therefore tends to suggest that modern poetry has these faults. Secondly, the argument lacks operational validity: if it suggests to people that Eliot, Pound, and Auden can be read in the same way as Shelley and

Keats, it misleads them seriously. (There is, of course, a genuine resemblance between some of Auden's verse and some of Byron's, but these are precisely those aspects of Byron that are not typically Romantic.) In this respect, Brooks is a safer guide: Donne is a good preparation for Auden.

After Spender's, the next two essays, both dating from the mid-Fifties, present the judgments of distinguished American women and men of letters on Auden's work. Marianne Moore's essay is of interest as the opinion of an American poet of the first rank, whose verse has had a distinct influence on some of Auden's later work, especially that in syllabic meter. She belongs to no critical school or trend, but displays the reactions of her own fine sensibility and keen intelligence to a kind of poetry very different from her own. Edmund Wilson, perhaps the best-known American critic and man of letters, takes a favorable view of the effect of Auden's translation to America on his work, in strong contrast to most English views of the same event.

The essay by John Bayley begins another group of three by British critics. Although I have expressed some reservations about the general thesis of Mr. Bayley's book, his discussion of Auden seems to me remarkably fresh and perceptive, and his emphasis on Auden's humanity and interest in the gossipy minutiae of ordinary life and people is a valuable corrective of the picture some critics give of him as inhumanly detached and abstract. His placing of Auden in the English and Dickensian tradition and his statement that Auden "owes more to Scott and Hardy than to Kierkegaard" are welcome and sane. I regret only that it was impossible to include Mr. Bayley's whole discussion of Auden, especially his sympathetic treatment of the *Age of Anxiety*. G. S. Fraser, who earlier did some excellent specific analyses of particular poems of Auden in *The Modern Writer and His World*,[8] presents an intelligent and informed view of Auden's whole career. Finally, Richard Hoggart's essay, though written as the introduction to a selection intended for sixth-form use in British schools, contains in brief compass Hoggart's latest interpretation of Auden's work as a whole. I have therefore chosen it in preference to an excerpt from his 1951 book, or one from his British Council pamphlet of 1957.

The essay by Carlo Izzo is included both for its intrinsic interest and as a specimen of Auden's reception in the non-English-speaking world. The first part of the essay is abridged from Izzo's introduction to his excellent

[8] G. S. Fraser, *The Modern Writer and His World* (London: Derek Verschoyle, 1953), pp. 230-66.

translation (with the English on the facing pages) of a selection of Auden's poems into Italian (1952); the rest is excerpted from his history of English literature (1963). In Germany Auden does not seem to have fared so well: both *For the Time Being* and *The Age of Anxiety* have been translated into German,[9] but the introduction to the first edition of the translation of *Age,*[10] by Gottfried Benn, whom one would have expected to find Auden congenial, was so ignorant and irrelevant that it was dropped from the later printing.

The concluding group of essays by American academic critics presents recent discussions in detail of some of Auden's major works. F. P. W. McDowell, in an excerpt from a longer essay, considers "The Sea and the Mirror"; Edward Callan, to whom students of Auden are indebted for his "Annotated Checklist" of Auden's works to 1958, discusses *New Year Letter,* and especially its relation to Kierkegaard; and Richard Ohmann relates Auden's recent critical volume, *The Dyer's Hand* (1962), to his earlier critical theory and to his poetry. Of my own book (1963), I will say only that I chose to excerpt the discussion of *For the Time Being* from it because this was a major work not considered at length in any of the other essays.

[9] *Das Zeitalter der Angst: Ein dramatisches Gedicht,* translated by Kurt Heinrich Hansen (Munich: R. Piper und Co. Verlag, 1958); *Hier und Jetzt; Ein Weihnachtsoratorium,* translated by Gerhard Fritsch (Salzburg: Otto Müller Verlag, 1961).

[10] *Das Zeitalter der Angst: ein barockes Hirtengedicht,* translated by Kurt Heinrich Hansen (Wiesbaden: c. 1947).

Some Notes on Auden's Early Poetry

by Christopher Isherwood

If I were told to introduce a reader to the poetry of W. H. Auden, I should begin by asking him to remember three things:

First, that Auden is essentially a scientist: perhaps I should add, "a schoolboy scientist." He has, that is to say, the scientific training and the scientific interests of a very intelligent schoolboy. He has covered the groundwork, but doesn't propose to go any further: he has no intention of specialising. Nevertheless, he has acquired the scientific outlook and technique of approach; and this is really all he needs for his writing.

Second, that Auden is a musician and a ritualist. As a child, he enjoyed a high Anglican upbringing, coupled with a sound musical education. The Anglicanism has evaporated, leaving only the height: he is still much preoccupied with ritual, in all its forms. When we collaborate, I have to keep a sharp eye on him—or down flop the characters on their knees (see "F.6." passim): another constant danger is that of choral interruptions by angel-voices. If Auden had his way, he would turn every play into a cross between grand opera and high mass.

Third, that Auden is a Scandinavian. The Auden family came originally from Iceland. Auden himself was brought up on the sagas, and their influence upon his work has been profound.

Auden began writing poetry comparatively late; when he had already been several terms at his public school. At our prep-school, he showed no literary interests whatever; his ambition was to become a mining-engineer. His first poems, unlike Stephen Spender's, were competent but entirely imitative: Hardy, Thomas and Frost were his models:

THE CARTER'S FUNERAL

Sixty odd years of poaching and drink
And rain-sodden waggons with scarcely a friend,

"Some Notes on Auden's Early Poetry" by Christopher Isherwood. From the "Auden Double Number" of *New Verse* (November 1937), 4-9. Reprinted by permission of the author.

Chained to this life; rust fractures a link,
So the end.

Sexton at last has pressed down the loam,
He blows on his fingers and prays for the sun,
Parson unvests and turns to his home,
Duty done.

Little enough stays musing upon
The passing of one of the masters of things,
Only a bird looks peak-faced on,
Looks and sings.

ALLENDALE

The smelting-mill stack is crumbling, no smoke is alive there,
Down in the valley the furnace no lead ore of worth burns;
Now tombs of decaying industries, not to strive there
Many more earth-turns.

The chimney still stands at the top of the hill like a finger
Skywardly pointing as if it were asking: "What lies there?"
And thither we stray to dream of those things as we linger,
Nature denies here.

Dark looming around the fell-folds stretch desolate, crag-scarred,
Seeming to murmur: "Why beat you the bars of your prison?"
What matter? To us the world-face is glowing and flag-starred,
Lit by a vision.

So under it stand we, all swept by the rain and the wind there,
Muttering: "What look you for, creatures that die in a season?"
We care not, but turn to our dreams and the comfort we find there,
Asking no reason.

The saga-world is a schoolboy world, with its feuds, its practical jokes, its dark threats conveyed in puns and riddles and understatements: "I think this day will end unluckily for some; but chiefly for those who least expect harm." I once remarked to Auden that the atmosphere of *Gisli the Outlaw* very much reminded me of our schooldays. He was pleased with the idea: and, soon after this, he produced his first play: *Paid on Both Sides,* in which the two worlds are so inextricably confused that it is impossible to say whether the characters are really epic heroes or only members of a school O.T.C.

Auden is, and always has been, a most prolific writer. Problems of form and technique seem to bother him very little. You could say to him:

"Please write me a double ballade on the virtues of a certain brand of toothpaste, which also contains at least ten anagrams on the names of well-known politicians, and of which the refrain is as follows. . . ." Within twenty-four hours, your ballade would be ready—and it would be good.

When Auden was younger, he was very lazy. He hated polishing and making corrections. If I didn't like a poem, he threw it away and wrote another. If I liked one line, he would keep it and work it into a new poem. In this way, whole poems were constructed which were simply anthologies of my favourite lines, entirely regardless of grammar or sense. This is the simple explanation of much of Auden's celebrated obscurity.

While Auden was up at Oxford, he read T. S. Eliot. The discovery of *The Waste Land* marked a turning-point in his work—for the better, certainly; though the earliest symptoms of Eliot-influence were most alarming. Like a patient who has received an over-powerful inoculation, Auden developed a severe attack of allusions, jargonitis and private jokes. He began to write lines like: *"Inexorable Rembrandt rays that stab . . ."* or *"Love mutual has reached its first eutectic. . . ."* Nearly all the poems of that early Eliot period are now scrapped.

In 1928, Spender, who had a private press, printed a little orange paper volume of Auden's poems. (This booklet, limited to "about 45 copies," is now a bibliophile's prize: the mis-prints alone are worth about ten shillings each.) Most of the poems were reprinted two years later, when Messrs. Faber and Faber published the first edition of their Auden volume: here is one of the few which were not:

Consider if you will how lovers stand
In brief adherence, straining to preserve
Too long the suction of good-bye: others,
Less clinically-minded, will admire
An evening like a coloured photograph,
A music stultified across the water.
The desert opens here, and if, though we
Have ligatured the ends of a farewell,
Sporadic heartburn show in evidence
Of love uneconomically slain,
It is for the last time, the last look back,
The heel upon the finishing blade of grass,
To dazzling cities of the plain where lust
Threatened a sinister rod, and we shall turn
To our study of stones, to split Eve's apple,

Absorbed, content if we can say "because";
Unanswerable like any other pedant,
Like Solomon and Sheba, wrong for years.

I think this poem illustrates very clearly Auden's state of mind at that period: in this respect, its weakness is its virtue. Auden was very busy trying to regard things "clinically," as he called it. Poetry, he said, must concern itself with shapes and volumes. Colours and smells were condemned as romantic: Form alone was significant. Auden loathed (and still rather dislikes) the Sea—for the Sea, besides being deplorably wet and sloppy, is formless. (Note "ligatured"—a typical specimen of the "clinical" vocabulary.)

Another, and even more powerful influence upon Auden's early work was non-literary in its origin—in 1929, during a visit to Berlin, he came into contact with the doctrines of the American psychologist, Homer Lane. (*Cf.* Auden's own account of this, in his *Letter to Lord Byron,* Part Four.) Auden was particularly interested in Lane's theories of the psychological causes of disease—if you refuse to make use of your creative powers, you grow a cancer instead, etc. References to these theories can be found in many of the early poems, and, more generally, in *The Orators.* Lane's teachings provide a key to most of the obscurities in the *Journal of an Airman* (Mr. John Layard, one of Lane's most brilliant followers, has pointed out the psychological relationship between epilepsy and the idea of flight).

The first collaboration between Auden and myself was in a play called *The Enemies of a Bishop.* The Bishop is the hero of the play: he represents sanity and is an idealised portrait of Lane himself. His enemies are the pseudo-healers, the wilfully ill and the mad. The final curtain goes down on his complete victory. The play was no more than a charade, very loosely put together and full of private jokes. We revised the best parts of it and used them again, five years later, in *The Dog Beneath the Skin.*

It is typical of Auden's astonishing adaptability that, after two or three months in Berlin, he began to write poems in German. Their style can be best imagined by supposing that a German writer should attempt a sonnet-sequence in a mixture of Cockney and Tennysonian English, without being able to command either idiom. A German critic of great sensibility to whom I afterwards showed these sonnets was much intrigued. He assured me that their writer was a poet of the first rank, despite his absurd grammatical howlers. The critic himself had never heard of Auden and was certainly quite unaware of his English reputation.

The scenery of Auden's early poetry is, almost invariably, mountainous. As a boy, he visited Westmorland, the Peak District of Derbyshire, and Wales. For urban scenery, he preferred the industrial Midlands; particularly in districts where an industry is decaying. His romantic travel-wish was always towards the North. He could never understand how anybody could long for the sun, the blue sky, the palm-trees of the South. His favourite weather was autumnal; high wind and driving rain. He loved industrial ruins, a disused factory or an abandoned mill: a ruined abbey would leave him quite cold. He has always had a special feeling for caves and mines. At school, one of his favourite books was Jules Verne's *Journey to the Centre of the Earth.*

A final word about Influences—or perhaps I should say, crazes. For Auden is deeply rooted in the English tradition, and his debt to most of the great writers of the past is too obvious to need comment here. The crazes were all short-lived: they left plenty of temporary damage but few lasting traces. The earliest I remember was for Edwin Arlington Robinson. It found expression in about half a dozen poems (all scrapped) and notably in some lines about "a Shape" in an Irish mackintosh which malice urges but friendship forbids me to quote. Then came Emily Dickinson. You will find her footprints here and there among the earlier poems: for example,

Nor sorrow take
His endless look.

Then Bridges published *The Testament of Beauty,* and Auden wrote the poem beginning: "Which of you waking early and watching daybreak . . ." which appeared in the first Faber edition, but was removed from later impressions. Finally, there was Hopkins: but, by this time, Auden's literary digestive powers were stronger: he made a virtue of imitation, and produced the brilliant parody-ode to a rugger fifteen which appears at the end of *The Orators.*

Auden's Imagery

by Cleanth Brooks

Many readers find modern poetry difficult, and difficult in a special sense. I am thinking not so much of the person who has read little poetry of any kind as of the man who has some acquaintance with the English classics. He is apt to find the modern English and American poets bewildering, and his knowledge of nineteenth-century poetry not only does not aid him but actually seems to constitute a positive handicap. What, for example, is he to make of a poem like the following?

> Sir, no man's enemy, forgiving all
> But will his negative inversion, be prodigal:
> Send to us power and light, a sovereign touch
> Curing the intolerable neural itch,
> The exhaustion of weaning, the liar's quinsy,
> And the distortions of ingrown virginity.
> Prohibit sharply the rehearsed response
> And gradually correct the coward's stance;
> Cover in time with beams those in retreat
> That, spotted, they return though the reverse were great;
> Publish each healer that in city lives
> Or country houses at the end of drives;
> Harrow the house of the dead; looking shining at
> New styles of architecture, a change of heart.*
>
> [—W. H. Auden]

If he recognizes in the phrase "a sovereign touch" a reference to the custom of the sovereign's touching for the king's evil, he still may wonder at the poet's motive in using the phrase. To compare contemporary

"Auden's Imagery." Excerpted, with the author's consent, from the chapters "Metaphor and the Tradition," and "Frost, MacLeish, and Auden," of *Modern Poetry and the Tradition* (Chapel Hill: University of North Carolina Press, 1939) by Cleanth Brooks, pp. 1-3 and 125-35.

* From *Poems* (1930), XXX; *Collected Poetry*, p. 110; *Collected Shorter Poems*, p. 120.

neuroses to a disease cured by a sovereign touch may seem overingenious, and perhaps unpleasant. Is poetry not to be sublime and elevating? Moreover, "sovereign" as used seems to come perilously near to a pun. But the pun, he knows, is the lowest form of humor; and yet, the poem is apparently a serious poem. The last line clearly demands a serious tone.

"The liar's quinsy" may also be puzzling. Why should a liar be described as a person suffering from quinsy? And why should the coward have a stance to be corrected? Is the coward being compared to an awkward athlete, and if so, why?

Moreover, the reader may feel some shock at the use of the word "spotted" in the sense of "located," "caught in the glare of the searchlight." Does not this use of "spotted" border on slang? What place does slang have in a serious poem? And what of the figure of the retreaters caught in the beam of the flashlight before they have got too far away and coaxed into coming back? Has the poet sufficiently prepared for it? Is it fair to expect the reader to grasp it at all? Or, if he does grasp it, are not the associations of such a figure out of tone in a poem which subsequent readings indicate is a prayer?

The reader brought up on nineteenth-century poetry may quite understandably conclude that the poet is writing with his tongue in his cheek, indulging in a private poke at the expense of the reader. For such a reader, the only apparent alternative is to conclude that the poet is incompetent, his own dupe.

In recent years several books have appeared which state the "common reader's" view, notably Eastman's *The Literary Mind,* Sparrow's *Sense and Poetry,* and Lucas' *The Decline and Fall of the Romantic Ideal.* Mr. Eastman is inclined, in most cases, to view the modern poet as being the dupe of his own theories; Messrs. Sparrow and Lucas, to regard him as somewhat more knowing and cynical. But they agree in finding much modern poetry to be unintelligible and in general unaccountable under any reasonable canons of the art.

The questions raised by Auden's poem, it is interesting to notice, are primarily questions of imagery. The poet uses comparisons which the reader feels are unpleasant or difficult or both. Some readers may feel that there are more important objections, but any reader who finds the poem unsatisfactory will almost certainly question the use of imagery, and perhaps begin by questioning the imagery. Moreover, he will recognize in such imagery a characteristic trait of much of the modernist poetry which bewilders him:

We are the eyelids of defeated caves.
[—Allen Tate]

. . . the evening is spread out against the sky
Like a patient etherized upon a table . . . .
[—T. S. Eliot]

And that a slight companionable ghost
Wild with divinity,
Had so lit up the whole
Immense miraculous house,
The Bible promised us,
It seemed a gold-fish swimming in a bowl.
[—W. B. Yeats]

What, in each case, is the poet trying to do? Such comparisons point to a mode of organization characteristic of modern poetry which to the common reader must seem illogical and puzzling. Our best point of entry into the problems raised by modern poetry would seem to lie here, in a consideration of the imagery.

* * *

If MacLeish represents the unprincipled sensibility, Auden represents, possibly, the sensibility fortified with principles, or perhaps, changing the viewpoint, the sensibility at the mercy of a set of principles—the artist working in the service of a cause. . . . At his best [Auden's] poetry reveals what we have called the structure of inclusion, with a maximum density and firmness and with no glib oversimplifications.

But there may be questions as to what is his best. The central impulse of Auden's poetry may be defined by quoting the last stanzas from Poem XX:

And all emotions to expression came,
Recovering the archaic imagery:
The longing for assurance takes the form

Of a hawk's vertical stooping from the sky;
These tears, salt for a disobedient dream,
The lunatic agitation of the sea;

While this despair with hardened eyeballs cries
"A Golden Age, a Silver . . . rather this,
Massive and taciturn years, the Age of Ice."

Auden's surest triumphs represent a recovery of the archaic imagery—fells, scarps overhung by kestrels, the becks with their pot-holes left by the receding glaciers of the age of ice. His dominant contrast is the contrast between this scene and the modern age of ice: foundries with their fires cold, flooded coal-mines, silted harbors—the débris of the new ice age. The advent of the new age of ice, a "polar peril," supplies the background for his finest poetry. In this poetry the archaic imagery is recovered—not as items of the picturesque but in the service of a fine irony. It is an irony which comprehends the poet himself and the class to which he belongs.

The poetry is thin in proportion as the irony tends to dissolve into external topical satire—e.g., "The Dance of Death"—not because it is topical, since his best poetry is often topical, but because the center is external to the poetry. In general, Auden's poetry weakens as he tries to rely upon an external framework—a doctrine or ideology.

The following passage, for instance, is an example of Auden's dominant theme and his most successful method: the satire is directed at an essential frivolousness of mind—a stodgy, comfortable, unconscious complacency which makes men disguise losses and injuries, or even accept them as a part of the natural order of things.

> It is later than you think; nearer that day
> Far other than that distant afternoon
> Amid rustle of frocks and stamping feet
> They gave the prizes to the ruined boys.
> You cannot be away, then, no
> Not though you pack to leave within an hour,
> Escaping humming down arterial roads. . . .

The sense of grim understatement native to the tradition of Old English poetry is used to point up mercilessly the desiccation of College Quad and Cathedral Close. "It is later than you think. . . ." (An English gentleman is never late to appointments—even the ruling classes will listen to an indictment couched in these terms, the poet implies.) "Nearer that day. . . ." (The description is ominously vague. Suffice it to say that it is not at all like that "distant afternoon" with its rustling of frocks and stamping of feet and the prize-giving. But the mention of the afternoon suggests what has brought to pass the day so different from it, and perhaps suggests also why the financier and his friends have lost their sense of time and do not realize the lateness of the hour.)

The phrase, "the ruined boys," is also menacingly vague. It means primarily boys ruined for living, boys moulded for other distant afternoons, not for that day, etc. But it suggests "sexually perverted," too, literally perhaps and certainly symbolically. They have been emasculated, made infertile and incapable of producing any healthy growth.

Perhaps the neatest effect of the grim humor is achieved in the last three lines where it is suggested that the descent of the whirlwind will find the gentlemen incapable of reacting even to catastrophe except in terms of their class and code. "Not though you pack . . ." (as for a weekend in the country. The gentlemen have had at least in their experience sudden invitations.)

But the final sardonic picture of the financier and his friends escaping in their saloon cars down arterial roads does not become flat and heavy-handed, for it is intimately related to the whole texture of the experience. The relationship between the elements in the passage is as intricate as in any other kind of poetry. The satire rises into a more serious mode.

This picture of spiritual decay finds its complement in the glimpses of the decayed industries of the North Country:

> Below him sees dismantled washing-floors,
> Snatches of tramline running to the wood,
> An industry already comatose,
> Yet sparsely living. A ramshackle engine
> At Cashwell raises water; for ten years
> It lay in flooded workings until this. . . .

This is the new ice age realized in terms of the land itself. The two pictures are constantly juxtaposed: on occasion, in a passage so brilliant as the following:

> Pass on, admire the view of the massif
> Through plate-glass windows of the Sport Hotel;
> Join there the insufficient units
> Dangerous, easy, in furs, in uniform
> And constellated at reserved tables
> Supplied with feelings by an efficient band
> Relayed elsewhere to farmers and their dogs
> Sitting in kitchens in the stormy fens.

The passage takes on, in view of the larger context of Auden's work, a symbolical character. The Alpine scene represents the remnants of Europe's last glacial period. The ruling classes use it as their playground; it is beautiful and safe, seen through the plate-glass windows of the luxury hotel. As representatives of the new ice age it is ironically appropriate that they should choose such a playground. They are part of the age: they are frozen—they have to be "supplied with feelings. . . ." But on another level of irony it is appropriate too: the new glaciers, not tame ones now, are to crush them.

The visitors at St. Moritz are contrasted with the farmers in their kitchens. The nexus is superficial; the farmers in the stormy fens have in common with the visitors merely the fact that they are listening to the same music, via radio. But the suggested connection is deeper. We are really dealing with understatement. That which the radios imply—the whole technical-industrial age—binds the two groups very tightly together indeed. The ruling classes are really being very foolish in ignoring the other classes. The term "stormy" is applied to the fens, but the suggestion carries over to the farmers too: they represent the storm which will overwhelm the top-heavy civilization. And the term "fens" itself takes place in the irony. The visitors at St. Moritz would do well to look for the new glaciers, not in the Alpine mountains—these do not matter—but in the last place one would think to look—the stormy fens.

If the account just given seems overingenious, one need not insist on it. Least of all do I intend to imply that the sets of contrasts were *consciously* contrived by the poet, or that the reader, in order to understand the poem, must work out such an analysis. But if one attempts to explain the added fullness and solidity of much of Auden's best work, he is driven back on such accounts as this: the connections which lace together the various parts of the poem, on inspection, become more and more complex; the symbolism, more and more rich; the analogies and contrasts, more and more detailed.

Certainly, it is the use of sharp contrasts which gives vitality to Auden's verse. It is by way of becoming a hallmark of his poetry. Obviously, it is a device which can be overworked, and in the verse of many of Auden's followers and in some of the weaker verse of Auden himself, it has become a stereotype.

The temptation to use shocking contrasts is particularly strong when satire is directed at smugness and complacency. The real criticism is, however, to be directed not at the degree of shock but at the fact that often in such verse the shocking and discordant is used merely for its own sake. In the passages dealt with earlier, as we have seen, the contrasts are involved in the central pattern: they are not aimless or irresponsible but are legitimate extensions from a center which they illuminate. Auden is not always so careful: the center to which the satire refers is sometimes negligible or confused. Take the following passage, for example (which, by the way, seems to owe something to Lindsay's "Bryan, Bryan, Bryan, Bryan"):

> Hearing the arrival of his special train,
> Hearing the fireworks, the saluting and the guns,
> Bob and Miss Belmairs spooning in Spain,
> Where is the trained eye? Under the sofa.
> Where is Moxon? Dreaming of nuns.
> Their day is over, they shall decorate the Zoo
> With Professor Jeans and Bishop Barnes at 2d a view,
> Or be ducked in a gletcher, as they ought to be,
> With the Simonites, the Mosleyites and the I.L.P.

In fairness to the poem, Auden is consciously using a method of broad satire with its complement, obviously exaggerated praise, in order to set up the positive matter which he means to convey, and which comes, with a change of tone, in a short passage at the end of the poem. Even so, the method is coarser, easier, than that used in the earlier passages commented upon.

The satire is broader still in sections of "The Dance of Death," where the poet relies more heavily on the external framework—and the external doctrine—to pull the poem together. The gain in clarity is immense, but the gain is at the expense of the poetry, as a comparison with some of the poetry in the more obscure "Paid on Both Sides" and "The Orators" will demonstrate.

It is some of Auden's disciples, however, whose work represents a real abuse of the use of contrasts. Mere contrast, obviously, becomes monotonous, and a continual dealing in heterogeneity soon becomes as flat as the collecting of resemblances. To fall into mere heterogeneity is the temptation of the poet who wishes to portray disintegration.

Oddly enough, it may be used with the same vagueness to portray the antithesis of disintegration, lusty growth. Whitman, for example, often uses heterogeneity for this purpose. In the catalogue passages we are given hunks of American variety:

> The mate stands braced in the whale-boat, lance and
> harpoon are ready,
> The duck-shooter walks by silent and cautious stretches,
> The deacons are ordain'd with cross'd hands at the
> altar,

> The spinning-girl retreats and advances to the hum of the big wheel,
> The farmer stops by the bars as he walks on a First-day loaf and looks at the oats and rye,
> The lunatic is carried at last to the asylum a confirm'd case. . . .

The heterogeneity is used by Whitman to celebrate formlessness. The tone asks us to note how tremendous, how various the continent is, and the discords are ironical at the expense of categories of any kind. The implication is that any classifications which one possesses are made to seem shabby and inadequate when called in to take account of the enormous teeming variety of the new country.

But the game is too easy for Whitman as the proponent of nebulous bonhommie and fraternity. The poetry is thin and diluted. The game is too easy also for the celebrants of a rather vague communism—or in their negative and satiric mode, the mockers at vague confusion and disintegration.

Auden shows his superiority by his ability to assimilate the discords into a meaningful pattern. In this connection it may be well to comment on the extent to which Auden has relied constantly on a method of assimilation and synthesis. The method has resulted in charges of obscurity —some of them quite justified, many of them unjustified; but it is this method which essentially makes him a far better poet than poets often linked with him, Day Lewis and Stephen Spender. Indeed, the faults of these two poets are the result of oversimplification. Lewis, in his weaker moments, furnishes obvious cases of a flat didacticism; Spender, of sentimentality. Auden, on the contrary, even in his less tightly knit verse, works continually in a pattern of synthesis, and the ambiguity as to his attitude is a function of this pattern.

For example, note the ambivalence of his attitude toward the English public school. In some of the poems, it is the nursery of English complacency; in others, the system—the schoolmaster's advice, the Rugby team—is accepted to be made the vehicle of the poet's statement. There is, of course, no real contradiction, but the attitude in which the apparent contradictions are resolved is far more complex than blanket acceptance or rejection. To give some instances, the poet is allowed to parody the schoolmasterish style, and to develop a tone of ragging, scolding, cheering up, coaxing, which fits his purpose admirably. The real seriousness of his advice is protected from oversolemnity by the fact that its expression is an obvious parody of boy-scoutism. This is to put it crudely, but consider:

> Do you think that because you have heard that on
>   Christmas Eve
> In a quiet sector they walked about on the skyline,
> Exchanged cigarettes, both learning the words for "I
>   love you"
>   In either language:
> You can stroll across for a smoke and a chat any eve-
>   ning?
>   Try it and see.

On one level, the passage represents a debunking of the heroism and chivalry of war; but on another, it is a statement of the seriousness of taking sides in a conflict which is much too grim for such fraternizing. On one level, it stands as an ironical parody of the tone of the school-master to the pupil or the veteran to the recruit; but in addition, it has its measure of seriousness (and is the more serious because the poet has shown himself conscious of the ludicrous aspects of such advice).

The many passages in Auden which deal with the devoted band of conspirators function in much the same way. Some seem to be parodies, ironical and sometimes pitying, of fascism; and others seem to be fantasies which contain hints of what the proper sort of fascism (revolutionary communism?) ought to be. The constantly suggested connection between the school gang and the fascist conspirators is really intricate and important. The poet is allowed to imply: fascism is juvenile—ought to appeal really to school boys. And yet he also is allowed to imply: these appeals have their validity—there is sloth and complacency which are to be combatted. I am far from suggesting that Auden wavers in his political views or that he is indifferent to political views. I am concerned to show that his attitude is one which accommodates in a dramatic unity the various elements which in our practical oversimplification are divided and at war with one another.

This quality is Auden's best certification as a first-rate poet though it will hardly recommend him to propagandists of one sort or another, or to proponents of an immediate cause. (It is interesting that he has already been called a fascist by at least one of the sterner American left-wing magazines.) The proponent of the cause will prefer to the complexity of drama with its real conflicts the knocking over of a straw man—will prefer to Poem XVI, "The Dance of Death" with its literal straw-man, the dancer, who can be ticketed and labeled.

But Poem XVI is fine enough to warrant a little further attention, and sections of it will furnish some of the best illustrations of Auden's positive virtues. The kind of unity which he achieves at his best is well illustrated by such a passage as the following:

> It is time for the destruction of error.
> The chairs are being brought in from the garden,
> The summer talk stopped on that savage coast
> Before the storms, after the guests and birds:
> In sanatoriums they laugh less and less,
> Less certain of cure; and the loud madman
> Sinks now into a more terrible calm.
>
> The falling leaves know it, the children,
> At play on the fuming alkali-tip
> Or by the flooded football ground, know it—
> This is the dragon's day, the devourer's. . . .

The poetry recommends itself at once by a certain fullness and richness of tone and by the organic quality of the rhythm. But if we are to be more precise we shall have little difficulty in showing how the contrasts among the various items serve to build up the quiet but powerful irony which is achieved. The chairs are brought in because it is the season of storms, but, as stated in the poem, it is suggested that this simple act is a reaction to the threat of destruction. The classes who can afford the gardens can make only trivial responses. They can view the "destruction of error" as only a storm to be avoided by seasonal migration. There is another irony in the fact that the "savage coast" has attracted the gentle folk because it *is* savage—with the conventional associations of the romantic and the picturesque.

Further lines of resemblance emerge on inspection: The summer hotel is a sort of sanatorium, at least in the lightest sense of the world "recreation." The summer talk of the hotel is thus allied with the laughter of the patients in the sanatorium; and to the madman's ravings, for the asylum is still another kind of sanatorium.

The summer talk, the patients' laughter, and the cries of the madman are ironically linked together in an insight which involves the nature of the whole civilization, an insight which sets up a new relation among aspects of civilization which are usually regarded as discordant and antithetical.

In the same way consider the relationship of the images in the section which follows. The children are like the falling leaves, natural—in a sense in which the fuming alkali-tip is not "natural," and yet it is natural that the children should play upon it. They have no place but the industrial rubbish heaps on which to play. The children pull it into the relevant world of the poem. The fuming alkali is a significant part of the world upon which the storm is to descend, and for which the visitors at the summer hotel are responsible, whether or not they care to acknowledge it. The children with their innocent play do acknowledge it, and in a sense know what is to occur as the adults of the ruling classes do not.

Moreover, the reference to the children prepares for and acclimatizes the dragon reference. Children believe in dragons as adults do not, and ironically, therefore—as well as literally—it is appropriate that it should be they who know that the dragon's day is at hand. As these ironies develop, further relationships emerge: the children, the madman, the sick, the leaves become related in their sharing of a knowledge which, ironically, is withheld from the mature, the sane, the healthy, and the human.

It is quite idle at this time to try to predict Auden's future career. His best work revolves around one rather narrow theme. Other themes will undoubtedly bring their special problems. What it does seem relevant to insist on here, and especially relevant in connection with the principles argued in this book, is that Auden's best poetry represents the structure which we discussed in the first chapters of this study.[1]

[1] An excerpt from Mr. Brooks's first chapter constitutes the beginning of the present essay.—*Ed.*

W. H. Auden and His Poetry

by Stephen Spender

I

The odd impersonality of W. H. Auden always gives his poetry, even when he shows the deepest insight into the human heart, an air of strangeness. It was this too which made him seem strange to his contemporaries when we were at Oxford. As an undergraduate Auden was outstanding not only for the excellent poems which he had already written, but for his habit of analyzing the lives of all his friends and fitting them into a psychoanalytic pattern around him. He was didactic, dogmatic, and extremely amusing, though in a buffoonlike way, with a gift of parodying himself rather than with Latin wit. As a very young man, dogmatic by temperament and yet holding no metaphysical or moral beliefs whatever, he seemed sometimes divided between using his undoubted powers over his fellow undergraduates in a Mephistophelean or in a benevolent way. As an undergraduate he was clever enough to be bad and wise enough to be good—wisdom, indeed, was his outstanding quality, although going hand in hand with a good deal of silliness—so he decided to play a benevolent role in other lives.

Already, at the university, Auden's relationships with his fellow beings had fallen into a pattern. They were really of two kinds—teacher-to-pupil and The Colleagues. Those of us who automatically fell into the role of pupil went to him for instruction about poetry, our psychological ailments, the art of living, and so on. The Colleagues—consisting pre-eminently of Christopher Isherwood (at Cambridge), Day Lewis, and Rex Warner—were a little group (sometimes called "The Gang") who were rather like a shadow cabinet, the successors to the literary heritage of tomorrow. There was quite a feeling of there being literary governments at this time: we were governed—it seemed—by J. C. Squire and

"W. H. Auden and His Poetry" by Stephen Spender. From *The Atlantic Monthly*, CXCII (1953), 74-79. Copyright 1953 by The Atlantic Monthly Company, Boston, Massachusetts. Reprinted by permission of the author and *The Atlantic Monthly*.

a group of Georgian poets—more like a cricket team than literary figures. The honorable opposition was Bloomsbury, amongst whom could be loosely counted Virginia Woolf, E. M. Forster, and T. S. Eliot.

Auden had a grasp of the literary politics of the contemporary scene which astonished me: for I was still at the stage of indiscriminate gaping admiration for whoever had published a book or poem. I think that Auden at a later stage has definitely renounced literary politics, and his interest in them was part of his curious playing around with sophisticated things when he was young.

Auden held certain views very strongly at Oxford. These have impressed themselves on me the more because he reversed most of them shortly after he left. Here are a few of his characteristic pronouncements:

A poet must have no opinions, no decided views which he seeks to put across in his poetry.

Above all, poetry must in no way be concerned with politics.

Politicians are just lackeys and public servants whom we should ignore.

The subject of a poem is only a peg on which to hang the poetry.

A poet must be clinical, dispassionate about life. The poet feels much less strongly about things than do other people.

Poems should not have titles.

Never use exclamation marks, and avoid abstractions.

At this time Auden was convinced that modern poetry should not be written in conventional verse patterns.

Almost the most frequent word in his vocabulary was "symptomatic." This could be used as a term of praise or as diagnosis. For example, the poetry of Eliot was excellent because it was "symptomatic," but a hesitancy of speech was also "symptomatic" of some psychological regression.

The external appearances of Auden's life have changed less than those of any other of my friends in the twenty-odd years which separate his rooms at Christ Church, Oxford, in 1930 from those in Greenwich Village today. At Oxford his rooms were kept tidy by a college scout and scout's boy (who whistled on the stairway a Mozartian tune composed by Auden which he had heard him playing on the piano). Auden's furniture was suited to rooms in an expensive college; his books were neatly set up on their shelves. He had days of dandyishness when he was well brushed and dressed. Today his rooms are untidy and the books lie upright, longways, or diagonally on the shelves. However, the rooms are those of the same person leading the same kind of life—the life of an undergraduate who remains a student even when he becomes poet and professor.

Yet Auden's ideas have changed as strikingly as his way of life has remained the same. There is a dualistic idea running through all his work which encloses it like the sides of a box. This idea is Symptom and Cure. Sometimes Auden's poems are more symptomatic than curative; sometimes they concentrate with an almost salvationist zeal on the idea of a cure. But from the early "look shining at /New styles of architecture, a change of heart," to the concluding lines of *The Age of Anxety:*

> In our anguish we struggle
> To elude Him, to lie to Him, yet His love observes
> His appalling promise . . .

the preoccupation is the same. The symptoms have to be diagnosed, named, brought into the open, made to weep and confess, that they may be related to the central need of love, leading them to the discipline which is their cure. The symptoms which prove that man needs to love and that "the grossest of his dreams is /No worse than our worship which for the most part /Is so much galimatias to get out of /Knowing our neighbour" have changed very little. The diagnostician Auden is much the same as he was at Oxford.

It is his conception of the Cure which has changed. At one time Love, in the sense of Freudian release from inhibition; at another time a vaguer and more exalted idea of loving; at still another the Social Revolution; and at a yet later stage, Christianity. Essentially the direction of Auden's poetry has been towards the defining of the concept of Love.

II

Auden starts out on this poetic journey from the negative, amoral, neutral position of the Oxford, clinical Auden. This early poetry, which expresses a complete detachment and attains a kind of frigid, clipped beauty, is not so much "art for art's sake" as "art for science's sake." The poet creates poems out of his observations, emotions, and literary influences, as though he were working in a laboratory. His skill conceals a defect which he has never entirely overcome—a lack of the sense of the inner form of a poem. By this I mean that with Auden form hardly ever seems to grow out of the experience which is the center of the poem, out of what Henry James would call its "felt life." The form is imposed from the outside by the force of a didactic idea or by those stanza patterns in which the later poet shows such virtuosity. But the earlier poems are often made up largely of scraps of still earlier ones of which he has preserved the best lines. It always seemed strange to me that he was not shocked at the idea of tacking lines from a rejected poem onto a new one—as though a poem were not a single experience but a mosaic held together by the consistency of an atmosphere, a rhythm, or an idea common to all its parts.

The Orators, published in 1932, contains the most uninhibited, high-spirited, and self-revealing work of the young Auden. There are two elements more developed than in the previous poems: savage humor and a more purposively directed use of psychoanalysis.

The Orators is also Auden's most English book. The theme is, as usual, the diagnosis of symptoms and the prescription of a cure, in answer to the question stated in the opening prose poem, "Address for a Prize Day": "What do you think of England, this country of ours where no one is well?" There follows a destructive analysis of the golf-playing, church-going, tea-drinking, Boy Scoutish, eccentric English middle class, in which Auden scoffs at the self-love, frustration, inhibitedness, and so on, of schoolmasters, parsons, spinsters, and gentry. The force of the poem is as a kind of agnostic prayer—stated in a buffoonish manner but nonetheless powerfully sincere—against self-deception, the denial of life-forces by frustrating conventions, and on behalf of an open conspiracy of living in which love, whether social, personal, or sexual, is the stated aim of living. Auden here puts himself on the side of Blake, D. H. Lawrence, and other English mystics, with their highly individualistic philosophies, who spent their creative energy in protesting against the smugness of England. Their protest comes from a bitter love of their country and a deep faith that a New Jerusalem could be built on this island if only the English would stop being so English.

The young Auden explored very thoroughly the negative and positive aspects of his agnosticism. On the negative side, he was ruthlessly and maliciously destructive. Judging everything by his standard of uninhibited truth as the aim towards which human relationships should be directed, he is equally merciless to society and individuals when they do not achieve this. Some early poems read like gloating over the destruction of the society into which the poet was born. Even when he is a good deal older he can write with a certain callousness in portraying the suffering of the inhibited. "Miss Gee" is a ballad in which the poet really appears to take pleasure in contemplating the death of a spinster from cancer: she has not loved or been loved, so she gets what's coming to her, seems to be his attitude in a poem which can hardly seem amusing to readers who have known or loved someone suffering from this disease. Auden has sympathy for those who wish to be cured, but little or none for the incurable.

There is in fact a flaw of feeling in his early work. He is intellectually over- and emotionally underdeveloped. Hence the schoolboyish ruthlessness of certain passages in *The Orators,* and hence also a disconcerting facility in allowing his intellect to lead him where it will, which has never left him. When, early in 1950, Auden together with other intellectuals answered a questionnaire about his religious beliefs, he alone of all those who answered seemed to experience no difficulty in accepting the strictest dogmas of the Christian faith. Reading his answers, I had the impression that he could so easily believe things that are almost incredible to many people because the Christian faith was to him the premise of a hypothesis explaining human behavior—just as, at another time, Freud's theories had been.

But if Auden is overintellectual, his intellect is critical of its own processes, and it is directed by a benevolent will. The danger of the intellectual is to establish himself, slightly disguised, as God, in the center of his own work. The early poem, "Since you are going to begin today," where the poet suddenly switches from the contemplation of a lover to an evolutionary view of human existence, reveals this danger; and it is enormously to Auden's credit that it was a danger of which he was aware. His problem always has been to discover an authority for the dazzling marginal commentary on existence which is his poems, which is not just himself or himself interpreting the views of Freud, Marx, and others. In the poems he wrote during the middle 1930s we can see him seeking such an objective authority in the idea of Love, invoked in poem after poem as the solution of all human problems, and yet not identifiable with God. The opening prologue to the collection *On This Island* is an invocation of just this force in the universe in the lines beginning:

> O love, the interest itself in thoughtless heaven,
> Make simpler the beating of man's heart.

Love is, then, a luminous center within which relationships are simplified. It is the "cure" for the individual and for society. Yet the inadequacy of such an abstract ideal must have dissatisfied Auden, making him seek the workings out of the tasks of love within the social movements of his time.

III

The central religious problem of his work was to some extent shelved (as happened with nearly all the serious writers of the 1930s) by political activities which pressed on intellectually in that decade.

Shortly after he had left Oxford in 1929, Auden traveled in Germany. The impression made by the Weimar Republic is already to be felt in the early poems. It is on the one hand of a society disintegrating "in the explosion of mania"; but on the other the Weimar Republic also meant youth, nakedness, lack of inhibitions, pleasure—everything which England banned.

Funds ran low, and Auden was forced to leave Germany and look for a schoolmastering job in England. This was not just a measure taken for financial reasons: it was also a recall to what he had always considered part of his vocation—teaching.

Schoolmastering proved a great success, and perhaps the years in the early 1930s when he was first at Helensburgh in Scotland, and later near Malvern in England, teaching at preparatory schools were the happiest of his life. At all events they produced his most harmonious poems. The beautiful poem beginning "Out on the lawn I lie in bed" (called "A Summer Night 1933" in *Collected Poems*), has a Midsummer Night's Dream quality which he never achieved before or since. The symptom-cure theme becomes woven here into the healing calm of a summer night:

> Now North and South and East and West
> Those I love lie down to rest;
> The moon looks on them all:
> The healers and the brilliant talkers,
> The eccentrics and the silent walkers,
> The dumpy and the tall.

One of Auden's characteristics is to make a cult of whatever he happens to be doing, which becomes to him what the poet must do. This self-culture or self-cultifying can be annoying, but we must accept it, to use Montherlant's phrase, as "the noble self-absorption" of a poet of genius. It is one aspect of a kind of concentration whereby the poet sanctifies whatever he does with his own presence, so that his environment becomes mythical just because he happens to be there. Thus Auden's poems when he is in Helensburgh acquire a certain Scottishness (owing something, incidentally, to Burns) and in Malvern they have a lush West of England quality. Auden never becomes a regional poet: rather he haunts the locality where he may be living at a given time, with a kind of local blessing derived from his presence.

A mixture of literary success, the anti-Fascist movement, and wanderlust took Auden away from schoolmastering. Early in 1937 he was in Spain as an ambulance driver or stretcher-bearer on the Republican side. Before this, he went on a summer holiday (which resulted in a book called *Letters from Iceland*) with Louis MacNeice. Later he went with Isherwood to China, with whom he wrote another book, *Journey to a War.* On their return from China, Auden and Isherwood first went to America, and it was at this time that they decided that this was the country where they wished to stay.

Another activity of these years was experimentation with the theater. Auden and Isherwood collaborated in writing *The Dog Beneath the Skin, The Ascent of F.6,* and *On the Frontier,* all of which were performed by an energetically directed group called The Group Theatre. Of these plays, *The Dog Beneath the Skin,* adolescent as its satire is, is perhaps the liveliest. It contains beautiful choruses thrown off by Auden, and some good lyrics. *The Ascent of F.6,* which describes a Himalaya expedition, comes nearest of these experiments to being a play. It is still successfully revived. *On the Frontier* is a hash of the revolutionary and pacifist thought of the 1930s, reduced to their least convincing terms. On the whole, the plays of Auden and Isherwood show little except the astonishing virtuosity of both writers, and a rather distressing overconfidence in what they can get away with. They seem to have liked the idea of collaborating, yet each seemed secretly resolved not to put his best efforts into a collaboration. The Auden-Isherwood plays provide considerable evidence that one aspect of the 1930s was a rackety exploitation of literary fashions.

IV

The effect of the turmoil of the 1930s on Auden's poetry was a tremendous inflow of new impressions, influences, and ideas, which he met with an ever-increasing virtuosity. Auden belonged more with his conscience than either with head or heart to the anti-Fascist movement of this time. He felt, as others did, that Fascism was wicked, political persecution a crime, the Spanish Republic the best cause of the first half of the twentieth century, and that unless the public could be awakened, war was inevitable. The 1930s were a perpetual state of emergency for those aware that there was an emergency. Thus Auden felt the pressure of the necessity of doing what he could to avert the war.

On the other hand, he disliked politics; he was bored by meetings, and still more by the spiritual condition which meetings signify, and he must have regarded the lives and attitudes of most of the people who were also anti-Fascists as shallow and tiresome. In his magnificent "Spain" he raised the level of the argument about Spain to a vision of past, present, and future, enclosed within the moment of struggle, which is the highest achievement of that epoch.

One reason why Auden could never rest content as a political Marxist lay in his complete rejection of the propagandist or class-interested view of truth. I remember meeting him shortly after I had attended the Writers' Congress in Madrid in the summer of 1937. I was disturbed at the time because so much of the energies of the *conférenciers* had been directed not against Fascism but against M. André Gide, on account of his recently published *Return from the U.S.S.R.* The argument most frequently used against Gide was not that his book was untrue, but that it gave comfort to the enemies of the Soviet Union. That sophistry of Marxist thought which justifies lies by arguing that all points of view are only the results of class interest, and that there is no such thing as "objective" truth, was brought to bear against Gide's book. At a time when many were uncertain what line to take, Auden comforted me enormously by his straightforward common sense. "Political exigency can never justify lies" was his comment on those who attacked Gide for revealing unpleasant truths.

The abruptness with which Auden dismissed any discussion justifying propaganda as a function of the "relativity" of truth confirms my impression that even his most arbitrary ideological positions are based on a recognition of salient facts. When I asked him in 1949 why he had ceased to be concerned with politics, he replied: "In the 1930s I thought that war could be stopped by opposing Fascism. We failed to do this, so I realized that subsequently nothing that I could do would be effective." In 1945, immediately after the war, he went for some weeks to Germany. When, on his return to America, he passed through London, I asked him whether he thought that the Occupation of Germany could achieve any good purpose. "Something might have been done, but it's too late," he answered.

Such statements may annoy intellectuals who are determined to think that they can play a role in politics even today, but are they not a recognition of the facts? It is facts which Auden arranges into the pattern of hypotheses which may strike the reader as fantastic. Facts are the original scraps of material which he puts into his transcendental kaleidoscope. Every line of his poetry—which has been called obscure—*means* something in the sense that it has an immediate relation to some real event which he interprets as a psychological or spiritual or sociological symptom. His poetry is, as I say, a brilliant commentary on our contemporary history, and to understand it one has to see what it is about, as well as enjoying the poetry. Although it has often a lyrical movement, it does not create the self-sufficient dream world, separated from living, of the romantic lyric.

If this poetry is difficult the difficulty arises from its being so packed with meanings that we do not recognize our impenetrable and largely insignificant environment in it. Auden's poetry is more intellectualized than the world as it really is. Every image he invokes signifies a symptomatic condition of society or individual psychology. There is a lack in his work of things which are just things—trees and stars and mountains and sun impenetrable in their own dazzling is-ness.

The great achievement of Auden is to use analyzable material creatively as a language of dream symbols and psychological fantasies directly related to the facts of our lives, in which he can depict our own history to us. Auden has developed the dream in poetry beyond the stage where the poet is passive dreamer. He does not go into a surrealist trance in which he makes his conscious mind an automatic machine for pouring out incomprehensible unconscious material: he consciously invents dreams and depicts actuality in the language of unconscious fantasies. In this way he has transformed the poetic role from that of the poet withdrawn into a world of wishful fantasies into that of the poet interpreting and creating dreams, writing a commentary on his epoch in a language of dream-fantasies and symbols. In lines like the following, one sees the fusion of the world of headlines, history, and power politics with that of dreams:

> Into this neutral air
> Where blind skyscrapers use
> Their full height to proclaim
> The strength of Collective Man,
> Each language pours its vain
> Competitive excuse:
> But who can live for long
> In an euphoric dream;
> Out of the mirror they stare,

Imperialism's face
And the international wrong.

Throughout the 1930s he provided a commentary on events which magically transformed public violence into the bogeys of personal fantasy. In this way he asserted what is perhaps the most difficult and important truth for people today to understand: that the public wrong can only be atoned and cured within the personal lives of individuals:

Hitler and Mussolini in their wooing poses,
Churchill acknowledging the voters' greeting,
Roosevelt at the microphone, Van der Lubbe laughing,
And our first meeting
But love except at our proposal
Will do no trick at his disposal. . . .

V

Auden's journey to America in 1938 was not, as it seemed to many people at the time, an escape from the consequences of the anti-Fascism which he had supported, but an attempt to rediscover his own isolation. Perhaps if he had remained in England, the different circumstances of the war would have been as great a change as the American scene for him, and he might have found that in the Blitz and at the time of the threatened invasion of Britain, the English did indeed experience the kind of simplification of all their purposes which he had prayed for ironically in *The Orators. The Double Man, The Sea and the Mirror,* and *The Age of Anxiety*—Auden's outstanding American works—are sustained attempts to reintegrate his thought after the disintegrating social thinking of the 1930s.

On the level of theory, Auden's latest poetry has an air of finality about it. His problem has always been to shift the center of his dogmatic ways of regarding experience from himself to some objective authority, so that he himself becomes a part of what is judged, and not just the center of his own system. The Church provides him with this new center. From now on his poetry becomes an exercise in humility and in interpretation of an authority not his own, instead of being self-assertive.

However, there is still a question about Auden, as a poet, to which the Church's authority alone does not provide the answer. Is he a brilliant marginal poetic commentator on the contemporary scene? What strikes me more and more in reading Auden is that his poetry is like a commentary, footnotes, appendixes—observations surrounding the history of his time, more brilliant, dazzling, and amusing perhaps (like Gibbon's footnotes) than the book itself. For all these wonderful observations, epithets, illuminations, the poet seems to stand aside, outside experience, observing the performance of his own and other lives from the wings. Or if he appears, it is in a too humble role, identifying himself with the faults and weaknesses of those around him, but with a cunning humility which enables him to escape into anonymity:

> Faces along the bar
> Cling to their average day:
> The lights must never go out,
> The music must always play,
> All the conventions conspire
> To make this fort assume
> The furniture of home:
> Lest we should see where we are,
> Lost in a haunted wood,
> Children afraid of the night
> Who have never been happy or good.

"We," the poet writes, but is this "we" any more convincing than the "we" which a preacher uses when he seeks to identify his own knowledge with the blindness and ignorance of his flock, in order to lead them along the way of his own knowledge? With a preacher this is traditionally justified, but in poetry it becomes a kind of sleight-of-hand in which the poet is using the idea of "I" to express something really nonexistent in his poetry.

The "I" who frequently occurs in Auden's poetry is, except in a few rare poems of happiness (for example the Helensburgh poems), either an anonymous commentator or (as in the lines I have quoted) an abstraction—the person assumed to be the common multiple of the "we" sitting in the bar on Fifty-second Street.

It might be argued that in his love poems Auden enters into a more sensuous awareness of his own existence and that of others than his usual diagnosis of the human heart and human behavior as an array of symptoms fitting into an abstraction. But it is here precisely that the peculiar absence of his own personality in his poems and his unawareness of other existences simply as what they are acquire pathos and are even tragic. His most justly famous love poem has such beauty of lyric movement that readers do not perhaps look at it closely. Perhaps also modern readers are so used to love poetry being a negation rather than an affirmation of a relationship, that they scarcely pause to consider what Auden is saying. The poem opens:—

> Lay your sleeping head, my love,
> Human on my faithless arm;
> Time and fevers burn away
> Individual beauty from
> Thoughtful children, and the grave
> Proves the child ephemeral:
> But in my arms till break of day
> Let the living creature lie,
> Mortal, guilty, but to me
> The entirely beautiful.

The visible situation, the actuality which strikes the senses here, is conveyed in the first two lines. The beloved is sleeping, and therefore unconscious. This is important because the rest of the poem shows that the nature of this love is an operation of the imagination—or rather of the intellectual will—of the poet upon the passive, characterless form of the beloved. What is evoked is the force of an illusion which can be built up out of a momentary situation, not the conscious love of two people for one another. The second line half invites and half forewarns us of the fragility of love, with the ambiguousness of the word "human." The word "faithless" reinforces what is sinister about the idea of "human."

Other poets have expressed the idea of the ephemeral nature of love compared with eternity. But in doing so they have appealed to their faith in a mystery: that something permanent can be snatched by lovers out of the enormous spaces of time. The mystery lies in this being at the same time an illusion and not an illusion. It is an illusion in that time does indeed destroy all individuality. It is not an illusion in that, within time, two adult people fully aware of their need for one another and of their love are able to enter into the realest situation possible in human relationships: an act of naked and final recognition of one another's lives. This is for them perhaps the most valuable experience in life, because it is an escape from loneliness into their awareness of one another.

This is the opposite of the view in Auden's poem that love is the evocation of an illusion, a moment snatched from eternity, in the mind of *one person,* holding in his arms the passive form of his beloved. The kind of love in Auden's poems is really an expression of the wish for death—

the wish to die into a moment of happiness, which Keats expresses so often in his poetry—"And so live ever or else swoon to death."

I do not wish, however, to criticize Auden for writing adolescent love poetry. A poet must write the poetry he can write, and I do not believe that psychological immaturity prevents a poet writing great poetry. Still less do I wish to criticize him because he is not an egotist in his poems. That he is not egotistic, and that he does not attempt to express an autobiographic personality, I consider among his virtues. The point, though, which I wish to make is that his poetry is often depersonalized in the same way that a philosophic argument or an article in the newspapers exists simply as an argument or as information, so that the reader cannot identify himself with the situation out of which the writer is writing, even if he feels that his own situation is stated in it, and even if the writer writes in the first person singular. It is not a matter of pronouns or autobiography. It is something which one feels in many of Auden's best lines:

> Tomorrow, perhaps, the future: the research on fatigue
> And the movements of packers; the exploring of all the
> Octaves of radiation;
> Tomorrow the enlarging of consciousness by diet and
> breathing.

The poet is *outside* these lines in a way in which Eliot or Yeats is never outside his own poetry. It is this, I think, which gives Auden his extraordinary air of authority. We feel that a person with flesh and blood like our own is not really involved in what he is saying. It is also what makes him often seem unconvincing. We feel that the poet has arrived at these conclusions by a process of reasoning which is outside the reasoning of his blood.

It is for this reason that some of the best younger English writers—Dylan Thomas and W. S. Graham—write a poetry whose every line is infused with their sensuous presence. It is the reason why a much more intellectual poet than Auden—Empson—seems much more concrete in his poems. It explains why Auden's long poems are singularly weak in construction: because only a unified personality can hold a long poem together. But it suggests also that Auden may be the poet who is most adapted to the abrupt changes, the lack of any center, in our age. He has often the hypnotic power, within his changeability and his elusiveness, which in a different though perhaps parallel way has enabled the chameleonlike Picasso to dominate all other contemporary painting.

W. H. Auden

by Marianne Moore

We surely have in W. H. Auden—in his prose and verse—stature in diversity. It is instructive, moreover, to see in him the abilities he admires in others—the "capacity for drawing general conclusions," mentioned by him as "the extraordinary, perhaps unique merit" of de Tocqueville; and together with clinical attention to cause and effect, a gift for the conspectus. After speaking of de Tocqueville as a counter-revolutionary—i.e., one who has no wish to return to the condition which preceded revolution—he says, "The body knows nothing of freedom, only of necessities; these are the same for all bodies," and "insofar as we are bodies, we are revolutionaries; insofar, however, as we are also souls and minds, we are or ought to be *counter*revolutionaries." He feels that "The books of de Tocqueville belong together with Thucydides, the Seventh Epistle of Plato, and the plays of Shakespeare, in the small group of the indispensable."

Mr. Auden embodies in his work many gratitudes. His *New Year Letter,* addressed to Elizabeth Mayer—"This *aide-mémoire* . . ./This private minute to a friend"—constitutes a veritable reading list of those to whom he feels a debt, and—an even better compliment—he has adopted various of their idiosyncrasies, as in the dedication to *Another Time* he recalls Blake's

> Till I Will be overthrown
> Every eye must weep alone.

In the *New Year Letter,* he says that Blake

> . . . even as a child would pet
> The tigers Voltaire never met,

"W. H. Auden." From *Predilections* (New York: The Viking Press, Inc., 1955) by Marianne Moore, pp. 84-102. One of a series of commentaries on selected contemporary poets, Bryn Mawr, 1952.

he feels that he has a debt to young Rimbaud,

> Skilful, intolerant and quick,
> Who strangled an old rhetoric,

and he says,

> There DRYDEN sits with modest smile,
> The master of the middle style.

If by the middle style he means the circumspectly audacious, he too is possessed of it.

He directs a warm glance toward Catullus,

> Conscious CATULLUS who made all
> His gutter-language musical.

Nor is Mr. Auden himself too fettered to use "who," "he," "the," or "which" as an end rhyme. He sees Voltaire facing him "like a sentinel." He says, "Yes, the fight against the false and the unfair was always worth it." He feels a debt to

> HARDY whose Dorset gave much joy
> To one unsocial English boy,

and Shakespeare? One is

> . . . warned by a great sonneteer
> Not to sell cheap what is most dear.

"Only by those who reverence it, can life be mastered." There is a suggestion of *Murder in the Cathedral* about that; as about the following reflection from *A Christmas Oratorio,* "The Temptation of St. Joseph":

> Sin fractures the Vision, not the Fact; for
> The Exceptional is always usual
> And the Usual exceptional.
> To choose what is difficult all one's days
> As if it were easy, that is faith. Joseph, praise.

Mr. Auden has a fondness for the seven-syllable-line rhythm,

> Now the ragged vagrants creep
> Into crooked holes to sleep;

the rhythm of

> Where the bee sucks, there suck I:
> In a cowslip's bell I lie . . .

and "Shame the eager with ironic praise" recalls Pope.

We infer approval of Ogden Nash in "a stranded fish to be kind to" and "had he a mind to"; again, in "Are You There?":

> Each lover has some theory of his own
> About the difference between the ache
> Of being with his love and being alone.

Appreciative of others he can afford to be. He could never sound as much like others as others sound like him. His collected poems, moreover, constitute, as Louise Bogan says, "the most minute dissection of the spiritual illness of our day that any modern poet, not excluding T. S. Eliot, has given us." He is a notable instance of the poet whose scientific predilections do not make him less than a poet—who says to himself, I must know. In "The Walking Tour," he speaks of how

> The future shall fulfil a surer vow
>
> Not swooping at the surface still like gulls
> But with prolonged drowning shall develop gills.

Commenting on Maria Edgeworth's Letters, Cecilia Townsend says, "Without sorrow, the spirit dwindles."[1] "Why are people neurotic?" Mr. Auden asks. "Because they refuse to accept suffering." And in one of his *Cornelia Street Dialogues* with Howard Griffin, he says, "suffering plays a greater part than knowledge" in our acts of the will. One can say, "I *should do* this. Will I do it? A part of the mind looks on; a part decides. Also one must not discount Grace." Mr. Griffin says: "You mean supernatural intervention—the light that appeared to Saul on the road to Damascus?" Mr. Auden: "Not really supernatural. . . . It may be perfectly natural. It depends on intensification of normal powers of sensitivity and contemplation."

[1] *The Spectator*, October 3, 1931.

In an address to the Grolier Club (October 24, 1946), Mr. Auden said, "Without an exception, the characters in Henry James are concerned with moral choices. *The Beast in the Jungle* is . . . the shrinking of the subject's sovereign will from decisive choice. . . . The interest itself is in the freedom of the will. Deny this freedom . . . and your interest vanishes." We have a debt to Mr. Auden for this emphasis put on "denial of free will and moral responsibility" as "a recent feature of our novels." Why must we "see ourselves," he asks, "as a society of helpless victims, shady characters and displaced persons, . . . as heroes without honor or history—heroes who succumb so monotonously to temptation that they cannot truly be said to be tempted at all?" The thought of choice as compulsory is central to everything that he writes. "Of what happens when men refuse to accept the necessity of choosing and are terrified of or careless about their freedom, we now have only too clear a proof," he said in 1941. "The will, decision, and the consequences—there is no separating them." His "Star of the Nativity" (*A Christmas Oratorio*) says:

> Descend into the fosse of Tribulation,
> Take the cold hand of Terror for a guide;
>
> But, as the huge deformed head rears to kill,
> Answer its craving with a clear I Will;

"In War Time" makes emphatic

> The right to fail that is worth dying for.

Home is

> A sort of honour, not a building site,
> Wherever we are, when, if we choose, we might
> Be somewhere else, yet trust that we have chosen right.

And we have in the Notes to Part III of the *New Year Letter:*

> I'm only lost until I see
> I'm lost because I want to be.

We must make "free confession of our sins." Humility, alas, can border on humiliation. In the *New Year Letter,* alluding to great predecessors, he asks, "Who . . .

Is not perpetually afraid
That he's unworthy of his trade,

Who ever rose to read aloud
Before that quiet attentive crowd
And did not falter as he read,
Stammer, sit down, and hang his head?

"Cognition," he says, "is always a specific historic act, accompanied by hope and fear."

How hard it is to set aside
Terror, concupiscence and pride.

Sin, fear, lust, pride. "The basis of pride," Mr. Auden says in "Dialogue I," is to be found in "lack of security, anxiety, and defiance; . . . says pride can be defined as a form of despair." And in the *New Year Letter* he says to the Devil:

You have no positive existence,
Are only a recurrent state
Of fear and faithlessness and hate,
That takes on from becoming me
A legal personality,

We hoped; we waited for the day
The State would wither clean away,

Meanwhile at least the layman knows
That none are lost so soon as those

Afraid to be themselves, or ask
What acts are proper to their task,
And that a tiny trace of fear
Is lethal in man's atmosphere.

Aware that Aladdin has the magic lamp that "Can be a sesame to light," he says:

Poor cheated Mephistopheles,
Who think you're doing as you please
In telling us by doing ill
To prove that we possess free will.

We have this metaphor of missed logic again in *The Rake's Progress,* where Nick Shadow leads Tom astray by suggesting that he is freed by disregarding passion and reason and marrying a freak. Choice is open to us each, and in *The Sea and the Mirror,* Alonso says:

> Learn from your dreams what you lack,
>
> Believe your pain: praise the scorching rocks
> For their desiccation of your lust,
> Thank the bitter treatment of the tide
> For its dissolution of your pride,
> That the whirlwind may arrange your will
> And the deluge release it to find
> The spring in the desert, the fruitful
> Island in the sea, where flesh and mind
> Are delivered from mistrust.

Similarly, Sebastian says:

> O blessed be bleak Exposure on whose sword,
> Caught unawares, we prick ourselves alive!
>
> The sword we suffer is the guarded crown.

In his preface to *The Sea and the Mirror,* Mr. Auden quotes Emily Brontë:

> And am I wrong to worship where
> Faith cannot doubt nor Hope despair
> Since my own soul can grant my prayer?
> Speak, God of Visions, plead for me
> And tell why I have chosen thee.

"Happiness does not depend," he says, "on power but on love." "The person must begin by learning to be objective about his Subjectivity"; so that "love is able to take the place of hate." And in *A Christmas Oratorio:*

> The choice to love is open till we die.
>
> O Living Love replacing phantasy.

The patriot may then ("Epithalamion," *Collected Shorter Poems*)

Feel in each conative act
Such a joy as Dante felt
When, a total failure in
An inferior city, he,
Dreaming out his anger, saw
All the scattered leaves of fact
  Bound by love.

"The Meditation of Simeon" (*A Christmas Oratorio*) would have us see "the tragic conflict of Virtue with Necessity" as "no longer confined to the Exceptional Hero. Every invalid is Roland defending the narrow pass against hopeless odds; every stenographer is Brunhilde refusing to renounce her lover's ring which came into existence" through the power of renunciation; and, redefining the hero, Mr. Auden's introduction to the Brothers Grimm says: "The third son who marries the princess and inherits the kingdom is not a superman with exceptional natural gifts." He "succeeds not through his own merit, but through the assistance of Divine Grace. His contribution is, first, a humility which admits that he cannot succeed without Grace; secondly, a faith which believes that Grace will help him, so that when the old beggar asks for his last penny, that is, when humanly speaking he is dooming himself to fail, he can give it away; and lastly, a willingness . . . to accept suffering. . . . From tale after tale we learn, not that wishing is a substitute for action, but that wishes for good and evil are terribly real and not to be indulged in with impunity." But, in the "Journey to Iceland," Mr. Auden asks:

"Where is the homage? When
  Shall justice be done? O who is against me?
  Why am I always alone?"

"Aloneness is man's real condition," he says; and as for justice, "The artist does not want to be accepted by others, he wants to accept his experience of life, which he cannot do until he has translated his welter of impressions into an order; the public approval he desires is not for himself but for his works, to reassure him that the sense he believes he has made of experience is indeed sense and not a self-delusion." [2]

"Lonely we were though never left alone," he says. We see loneliness

[2] *Partisan Review,* April 1950, reviewing *The Paradox of Oscar Wilde* by George Woodcock. To Oscar Wilde, Mr. Auden says, "Writing was a bore because it was only a means of becoming known and invited out, a preliminary to the serious job of spellbinding."

"sniffing the herb of childhood" and finding home a place "where shops have names" and "crops grow ripe"; and "In Praise of Limestone" (*Nones*) he reminds himself of

> . . . rounded slopes
> With their surface fragrance of thyme and beneath
> A secret system of caves and conduits; . . .

indeed says,

> . . . when I try to imagine a faultless love
> Or the life to come, what I hear is the murmur
> Of underground streams, what I see is a limestone landscape.

In the essay on Henry James—already referred to—he also says, "It is sometimes necessary for sons to leave the family hearth; it may well be necessary at least for intellectuals to leave their country as it is for children to leave their homes, not to get away from them, but to re-create them"; adding, however, that "those who become expatriate out of hatred for their homeland are as bound to the past as those who hate their parents." Having, like James, left the family hearth, an exile—"to keep the silences at bay"—must "cage/His pacing manias in a worldly smile" ("Vocation," *The Double Man*). It is not, however, a case of wishing nothing to be hard.

"A problem which is too easy," Mr. Auden says, "is as unattractive as a problem which is senseless or impossible. In playing a game, the excitement lies not in winning but in just-winning, and just-losing is almost as good as winning, and the same surely is true for thinking." Alluding to superficial or hasty persons, he says in "Our Bias":

> How wrong they are in being always right.
>
> For they, it seems, care only for success:
> While we choose words according to their sound
> And judge a problem by its awkwardness.

"A favorite game of my youth," he says, "was building dams; the whole afternoon was spent in building up what in the end was destroyed in a few seconds."

As offsetting the tribulations of life and a sense of injustice, one recalls Wallace Stevens' emphasis on the imagination as delivering us from our "bassesse." This, poetry should do; and W. H. Auden quotes Professor R. G. Collingwood as saying, "Art is not magic, but a mirror in which others may become conscious of what their own feelings really are. It mirrors defects and it mirrors escape"—affirmed in "The Composer" (*Collected Shorter Poems*):

You alone, alone, O imaginary song,
Are able to say an existence is wrong
And pour out your forgiveness like a wine.

Thinking of W. H. Auden the person, one recalls the *Letter to Lord Byron:*

But indecision broke off with a clean-cut end
One afternoon in March at half-past three
When walking in a ploughed field with a friend;
Kicking a little stone, he turned to me
And said, 'Tell me, do you write poetry?'
I never had, and said so, but I knew
That very moment what I wished to do.

"He dramatizes everything he touches," Louise Bogan says—as in "Under Which Lyre" (*Nones*),

Our intellectual marines,
Landing in little magazines
Capture a trend.

He sees "The bug whose view is baulked by grass," and our discarded acts

Like torn gloves, rusted kettles,
Abandoned branchlines, worn lop-sided
Grindstones buried in nettles.

The recitative to *Night Mail*—the British documentary film on the non-stop express from London to Edinburgh—is drama without a break:

In the farm she passes no one wakes
But a jug in a bedroom gently shakes.

Poets are musicians, and Mr. Auden's "In Praise of Limestone" says that one's "greatest comfort is music," "Which can be made anywhere and is invisible"; unlike

> The beasts who repeat themselves, or a thing like water
> Or stone whose conduct can be predicted . . . .

A poet is susceptible to "elegance, art, fascination," and words demonstrate the appetite for them which made them possible:

> Altogether elsewhere, vast
> Herds of reindeer move across
> Miles and miles of golden moss,
> Silently and very fast.

That Mr. Auden is a virtuoso of rhythms we seen in Ariel's refrain, "I," to Caliban ("Postscript," *The Sea and the Mirror*)—rivaling in attraction Herbert's "Heaven's Echo":

> Weep no more but pity me,
> Fleet persistent shadow cast
> By your lameness, caught at last,
> Helplessly in love with you,
> Elegance, art, fascination,
> Fascinated by
> Drab mortality;
> Spare me a humiliation
> To your faults be true:
> I can sing as you reply
> . . . I [Echo by the Prompter]

And the next verse ends:

> I will sing if you will cry
> . . . I

And the last verse:

> What we shall become,
> One evaporating sigh.
> . . . I

Urgency of a different sort we have in "Many Happy Returns (For John Rettger)":

> I'm not such an idiot
> As to claim the power
> To peer into the vistas
>   Of your future, still
> I'm prepared to guess you
> Have not found your life as
> Easy as your sister's
>   And you never will.

"One Circumlocution" (*Nones*) masters the art of rapt celerity:

> Speak well of moonlight on a winding stair,
> Of light-boned children under great green oaks;
> The wonder, yes, but death should not be there.

Could the skill of the pauses be better, in "To You Simply"?

> Fate is not late,
> Nor the speech rewritten,
> Nor one word forgotten,
> Said at the start
> About heart,
> By heart, for heart.

And, superlatively accomplished, there is Poem XI in *Songs and Other Musical Pieces:*

> Lay your sleeping head, my love,
> Human on my faithless arm;
> Time and fevers burn away
> Individual beauty from
> Thoughtful children, and the grave
> Proves the child ephemeral:

The emphasis on "from" corroborates an impression that Mr. Auden is exceptional, if not alone, in imparting propriety to words separated from the words to which they belong. He has notably, moreover, a faculty for keeping a refrain from falling flat, as where in *A Christmas Oratorio* the Wise Men say, "Love is more serious than Philosophy"; reinforcing interior rhymes, we have intermittently the variant on "y" as a refrain —apathy, deny; tyranny, occupy; certainly, anarchy, spontaneity, enemy, energy, die; phantasy, by, and "Time is our choice of How to love and Why"—a device of great dignity.

As preface to his *Collected Poetry,* Mr. Auden says: "In the eyes of every author, I fancy, his own past work falls into four classes. First, the pure rubbish which he regrets ever having conceived; second—for him the most painful—the good ideas which his incompetence or impatience prevented from coming to much (*The Orators* seems to me such a case of the fair notion fatally injured); third, the pieces he has nothing against except their lack of importance; these must inevitably form the bulk of any collection since, were he to limit it to the fourth class alone, to those poems for which he is honestly grateful, his volume would be too depressingly slim."

Destined for the last category, surely, is *The Double Man*—particularly its *New Year Letter,* written in octosyllabic couplets with an occasional triplet, a diagnosis of the spiritual illness of our day and a landmark in literature. Here, as in the *Letter to Lord Byron,* Mr. Auden has chosen a form "large enough to swim in," and in it discusses our quest for freedom; we being—as epitomized by Montaigne on the title page— "double in ourselves, so that what we believe we disbelieve, and cannot rid ourselves of what we condemn." The Double Man asks (*New Year Letter* and Notes):

> Who built the Prison State?
> Free-men hiding from their fate.
> Will wars never cease?
> Not while they leave themselves in peace.

Therefore:

> The situation of our time
> Surrounds us like a baffling crime.
>
> Yet where the force has been cut down
> To one inspector dressed in brown,
> He makes the murderer whom he pleases
> And all investigation ceases.

"Peace will never be won," Mr. Dulles insists, "if men reserve for war their greatest effort"; as "we wage the war we are," Mr. Auden says; and not having waged it well, find ourselves waging the other kind also; from Spain to Siberia, from Ethiopia to Iceland; irresponsibleness having brought about

> The Asiatic cry of pain,
>
> The Jew wrecked in the German cell,
> Flat Poland frozen into hell.

We are in a "coma of waiting, just breathing," because of our acedia or moral torpor,

> And all that we can always say
> Is: true democracy begins
> With free confession of our sins.

"Dante . . . showed us what evil is; not . . . deeds that must be punished, but our lack of faith." For "volunteers," it is "the penitential way that forces our wills to be freed," hell's fire being "the pain to which we go if we refuse to suffer."

When liberty has been recognized as "a gift with which to serve, enlighten, and enrich," then man is not in danger of being "captured by his liberty"; girls are not "married off to typewriters," children are not "inherited by slums"; and instead of terror, pride, and hate, we have faith, humility, and love. Just now, however, "with swimming heads and hands that shake," we watch the devil trying to destroy the root of freedom—that "absence of all dualities" that grows from "the roots of all togetherness," for "no man by himself has life's solution." "The Prince that Lies," he who

> . . . controls
> The moral asymmetric souls
> The either-ors, the mongrel halves
> Who find truth in a mirror, laughs.

He "knows the bored will not unmask him." Mr. Auden is not bored and has here met the devil with a deadly and magnificent clarity. "The great schismatic . . . hidden in his hocus-pocus" has "the gift of double focus," but

> . . . torn between conflicting needs,
> He's doomed to fail if he succeeds,

If love has been annihilated
There's only hate left to be hated.

Understating his art as "The fencing wit of an informal style," Mr. Auden has taken a leaf from Pope and devised the needful complement whereby things forgot are henceforth known; and with the apparently effortless continuity of the whale or porpoise in motion, he evolves constantly entertaining treatment, resorting to varied terminology—Greek, Latin, English, or other—presenting what he has to say, with that crowning attraction, as he uses it, paradox at its compactest.

An enemy to primness, Mr. Auden sometimes requires that we enjoy "the Janus of a joke" at our expense, as when he relegates the feminine to Laocoön status:

Das weibliche that bids us come
To find what we're escaping from.

And he is laughing at us also when he rhymes "ideas" with "careers," "delta" with "skelter," and "Madonnas" with "honors."

It is sad that we should be "the living dead" beneath selfishness and ingratitude; that "few have seen Jesus," and so many "Judas the Abyss." Persuading us to "show an affirming flame" rather than "the negative way through Time," and to believe that the cure for either tribulation or temptation is humility, these New Year thoughts

Convict our pride of its offence
In all things, even penitence.

For we have here, despite much about the devil, a poem of love and things of heaven—with a momentum of which Buxtehude or Bach need not be ashamed, the melodic entirety being something at which to marvel.

Inconvenienced, aided, attacked, or at large; a wave-worn Ulysses, a Jerome among his documents; a misinterpreted librettist; or a publisher's emissary insistently offered at luncheon a dish of efts, Mr. Auden continues resolute. He has a mission. Kimon Friar says, "There is an impersonality, it seems to me . . . at the very center of Auden's style and thinking, a veritable Ark of the Lord in which may be housed the Holy Spirit or—to the unbaptized eye—state the matter in accordance with your nature." [3] Education and tribulation certainly have not been wasted

[3] *Poetry,* May 1944.

on Mr. Auden. His leaf does not wither; his technical proficiencies deepen. In "The Shield of Achilles," he says he saw

> A ragged urchin, aimless and alone,
> . . . who'd never heard
> Of any world where promises were kept,
> Or one could weep because another wept.

Even a tinge of "greed" makes him "very ill indeed." His studies of Henry James and of Poe show to what heights of liberality he can rise. As a champion of justice, he will always have a champion in the pages he has penned; and as the Orpheus of our mountains, lakes, and plains, will always have his animals.

W. H. Auden in America

by Edmund Wilson

It is interesting to go back over Auden's books and to try to trace the effect on his work of his residence in the United States, to which he first came in 1939 and which, now an American citizen, he has made his headquarters ever since. Let me say at the outset that this influence of America does not seem to me in the least to have diluted the Englishness of Auden or to have changed its essential nature. Auden's genius is basically English—though in ways which, in the literary world, seem at present rather out of fashion. He is English in his toughness, his richness, his obstinacy, his adventurousness, his eccentricity. What America has done for Auden is to help him to acquire what is certainly today one of the best things an American can hope to have: a mind that feels itself at the centre of things. It has given him a point of view that is inter- or super-national.

One can see now, in re-reading Auden, that he had always a much more widely foraging habit of mind than most English writers of his generation. The chief theme of his early work was, to be sure, a British schoolboy conspiracy in which the Marxist crusade against capitalism was identified with the revolt of the young against schoolmasters and parents and their governments. The economic crisis of the Thirties gave rise to such protests everywhere and inspired such subversive hopes, but the rebellion of Auden and his friends was so much in terms of the English world—of public-school, university and Bloomsbury—in which they had grown up and been educated and in which they now felt themselves imprisoned—as scarcely to be intelligible elsewhere. A brilliant poem such as the *Last Will and Testament* of Auden and Louis MacNeice, included in their *Letters from Iceland,* will need eventually as many notes to explain its innumerable references to the Oxford-Cambridge-London group as the Testaments of Villon that suggested it (though it should always

"W. H. Auden in America" by Edmund Wilson. From *The New Statesman and Nation,* LI (June 9, 1956), 658-59.

be able to speak for itself as the Testaments of Villon do). Yet there was more in this early Auden than the schoolboy loves and hates and the private jokes. The writer of this article, who first read Auden's poems at a time when he had seen very little of England since the beginning of the first world war in the summer of 1914, was largely unaware of their interest as a commentary on English life. It was only in 1945, when, returning to the United States after spending some time in England, he looked into these early poems of Auden again, that he found in them an illuminating picture of an England he had not known till he saw it, in a further phase, at the end of the second war: an England suburbanised, industrialised, considerably Americanised, impoverished and sadly crippled but pretending that nothing had happened. One could see how young men in England, in the years just before the war, might have thought they would be happier in the United States, where you had the whole thing on a bigger scale—the excitements of the machine age and its bankruptcies, the vulgarities as well as the freedoms of an era of social levelling—and with not so much of the past to act as a drag on new departures. Those who criticised Auden and his friends in the Thirties for not outgrowing their schoolboy mentality should not blame them for breaking away and betaking themselves to a country where hardly half-a-dozen names in the Iceland Testament would even be recognised. They had already begun to explore: Spain and Germany as well as Iceland. Auden and Christopher Isherwood had made, in 1938, a journey to Hongkong and Shanghai, then had crossed the Pacific to Vancouver and ended up in New York. They returned at that time to Europe, but the following year came back to live permanently here in the United States. With Auden the process of Americanisation had already begun in England. He had been reading American writers, had tried his hand at American ballads, and had shown, in these and in *The Dance of Death,* published in 1933, that he had already—in rather a surprising way—got the hang of the American vernacular.

The first fruits of Auden's American period—especially *New Year Letter* of 1941, which contains the long poem of that title and the sonnet sequence *The Quest*—are already in certain ways quite distinct from anything he had written in England. The poet is more alone. "Derek" and his other allies as well as "the enemy" of *The Orators* have disappeared in *The Quest.*

What is the greatest wonder in the world?
The bare man Nothing in the Beggar's Bush.

These strange *dépaysés* sonnets seem to me unique and enchanting—their fairy-like phantoms that alternate with commonplace down-to-earth phrases, their images that dilate or wobble, the mysterious concluding poem with its blur of beginnings and endings:

> The gaunt and great, the famed for conversation
> Blushed in the stare of evening as they spoke,
> And felt their centre of volition shifted.

It was in connection with *New Year Letter* that the writer of this article first noticed a certain characteristic of Auden's writing. If one was baffled by a passage in one of his poems, one was likely to become aware soon afterward that what the poet had been saying was something that, precisely, one had just felt oneself but that one had hardly expected to find expressed in poetry so promptly.

If the hero of *The Quest* seems stripped of old friends, the longer poem, *New Year Letter,* addressed to a refuge from Germany, opens on a larger vista than those of the earlier poems:

> Across East River in the night
> Manhattan is ablaze with light . . .
>
> More even than in Europe, here
> The choice of patterns is made clear
> Which the machine imposes, what
> Is possible and what is not,
> To what conditions we must bow
> In building the Just City now.

The last lines of this poem give voice to the poet's exhilaration in moving about the world and the conviction of solidarity with companions in anxiety everywhere that was justified by such a response on the part of the foreign reader as, in my own case, I have mentioned above:

> O every day in sleep and labour
> Our life and death are with our neighbour,
> And love illuminates again
> The city and the lion's den,
> The world's great rage, the travel of young men.

He touches here on American history, but he makes no attempt to talk American. He speaks of "East River" without the article, as no New

Yorker would do. One finds in the *Letter,* as in *The Quest,* an accent of loneliness. Yet one feels that the poet is now, as he was not in his earlier poems, a completely free-swimming organism; and he has created his extraordinary new language, a brilliant international English, which may drop into French or German or carry along bits of Latin and Greek, and which is presently to absorb much American. He is not here any longer rebelling against British institutions that have irked his boyhood. He is dealing with the whole modern world: its discomforts, its disquiets, its crimes, its myths—"the city and the lion's den"; with the problem of how to live in it, to get out of it what it can give, to avoid being paralysed or bought by it. It may well be that this aspect of Auden is more intelligible to an American than to an Englishman, for this feeling oneself a member of a determined resistant minority has been now for nearly a hundred years a typical situation in America. Such people in the later nineteenth century were likely to be defeated or embittered. In our own, they have felt the backing of a partly inarticulate public who are not satisfied with the bilge that the popular media feed them in their movies and magazines, and who are grateful to anyone who will make a stand for that right to think for themselves which is supposed to be guaranteed us by the Bill of Rights and that right to a high level of culture which the framers of the Constitution—taking it so much for granted—would never have thought to include. These American writers of which I speak do not constitute a group, they do not frequent an official café; and on this account, the visitor from Europe is likely to come to the conclusion that, except in the universities, we have no intellectual life. He cannot conceive that the American writers are functioning in the crevices of cities, on the faculties of provincial colleges or scattered all over the country in the solitude of ranches and farms. This kind of life was now to be Auden's lot, and he must have had some desolating experiences:

> Some think they're strong, some think they're smart,
> Like butterflies they're pulled apart,
> America can break your heart.
> *You don't know all, sir, you don't know all.*

But I have always been struck by the naturalness with which Auden took things here for granted and—though I thought there was a good deal he did not understand—with the perfect propriety of his being here. One felt this especially when one noticed how easily he was able to incorporate the American colloquial speech, American allusions and customs, into the marvellous amalgam of his language, along with his foreign quotations, his technical vocabulary of botany, psychology and metallurgy (that sometimes derail the reader) and all those toothsome old British words—such as *mawmet, faffle* and *balter*—than turn out, when you look them up, to be Prov. Eng. or Dial. Eng., Archaic or Obsolete. It is not a question here of a successful American impersonation, as in the case of those stories of Kipling's that are supposed to be told by Americans or of those parts of Isherwood's *The World in the Evening* in which the narrator's American aspect is supposed to be uppermost. Such performances are *tours de force,* in which the least slip will jar. But in Auden an "East River" or two does not matter, since it is not an imaginary American who is speaking—and even when Auden has assigned his lines to some invented being (he has little dramatic sense)—it is the language of Auden that is speaking, and this language has breathed in its Americanism as easily as its Oxford gossip, its country talk of *leats* and *eagres,* its Horatian and Anglo-Saxon metres. The poem called *The Unknown Citizen,* contributed to the *New Yorker* at an early stage of Auden's American residence, was a satire on standardisation of a kind of which we had already had a good deal and which it did not take Auden to give us; but by the time he did his Phi Beta Kappa ode for Harvard in 1946, he had a quite intimate knowledge of the special world to which he was addressing himself, and had something of his own to tell it.

It is curious to compare Auden in his London dress of the *Poems* of 1930, published by Faber & Faber, one of their thin and distinguished volumes that all the smart people read, with Auden in American homespun—or at least, in a New York suit—the *Collected Poetry* of 1945, published by Random House. Hardly can we recognise here the young man, just up from Oxford, who appeared, under Eliot's patronage, in company with a few select friends. The friends are no longer present; the poems that seemed to herald the British revolution—including some very good ones—have for the most part been pitilessly scrapped. We find a volume printed on not good grey paper, of over four hundred pages, in which the poems are all run together, not beginning on separate pages, and in which old poems have been given new titles of a colloquial, even folksy kind: *Please Make Yourself at Home, It's Too Much, Something is Bound to Happen, Venus Will Now Say a Few Words.* Here are most of our favourite old friends, along with a lot of new ones, sitting around in New York or strolling on the college campus. One saw with surprise that Auden—so far from being a rarity that could only be appreciated by a few—was the old-fashioned kind of poet, like Browning or Henry Wadsworth Longfellow (not that I would compare him with the latter), who is at his best when printed and read in bulk. He amuses us, converses with us, does his best to give us good advice; he sings us comic songs, supplies us with brilliant elegies on the deaths of great contemporaries; he charms us, he lulls us to sleep; he lifts us to a moment of inspiration. In metrics, in architectonics, as well as in handling of language, he is, of course, an incredible virtuoso—the most accomplished poet in English since the great nineteenth-century masters; Tennyson, Browning and Swinburne; he does not call attention to this, and many people who read him do not even know it. If he is not precisely a "family poet" like Longfellow, Wordsworth and Tennyson, the fact that he is one of the most edible, one of the most satisfactory of contemporary writers in verse is proved by the sales of the *Collected Poetry,* which have reached, in the United States, the almost unprecedented figure of over thirty thousand copies.

I have had lately a little the feeling that the interest for Auden of the United States is not now quite so lively as it once was. His last book, *The Shield of Achilles,* seems less localised than any of its predecessors. One of its most attractive features is the sequence of lovely *Bucolics* that consists—under such bald titles as *Mountains, Lakes, Islands* and so on—of generalised pieces about landscape, about landscape presented in a novel but very characteristic way that is at once geological and subjective. Since becoming an American citizen, the poet has not ceased to explore, to roam—he has covered more ground in this country than most Americans do, and he now spends every summer in Italy. This spring he returns to England to be lecturer on poetry at Oxford. It is a part of his role to go everywhere, be accessible to all sorts of people, serve interestedly and conscientiously in innumerable varied capacities: on the staff of a Middle Western college; at a cultural congress in India; on a grand jury in New York City, deciding the fate of gangsters; on a committee of the American Academy, making handouts to needy writers. He has above all withstood the ordeal of America through a habitation of seventeen years; he has even "succeeded" here. And he has made all these exploits contribute to the work of a great English poet who is also—in the not *mondain* sense—one of the great English men of the world.

W. H. Auden

by John Bayley

At the time of Yeats's final phase, Auden belonged to a group of poets whose aims were intimately connected with social and political questions; he was learned in psychology and anthropology; his approach was avowedly "scientific"—that is to say, detailed, enquiring, impartial; he believed that an artist should be "more than a bit of a reporting journalist"; he was in touch with all the latest ideas and the latest developments. Apparently, his whole approach to life and art could scarcely have been more different from that of Yeats. And yet as we read his poetry, and in particular the early volumes, we feel that the response we give them—and the response they appear to require—is not so different. Not that Auden renounces by implication what actually happens in most people's lives: on the contrary he is passionately interested in all the details. But the mechanism by which his poetry bites on to such material—rhetorical, self-confident to the point of arrogance, intent on securing the advantage of an immediate effect—all this is very like Yeats.

Get there if you can and see the land you once were proud to own
Though the roads have almost vanished and the expresses never run:

Smokeless chimneys, damaged bridges, rotting wharves and choked canals,
Tramlines buckled, smashed trucks lying on their side across the rails;

Power-stations locked, deserted, since they drew the boiler fires,
Pylons falling or subsiding, trailing dead high-tension wires;

Head-gears gaunt on grass-grown pitbanks, seams abandoned years ago;
Drop a stone and listen for its splash in flooded dark below. . . .

These were boon companions who devised the legends for our tombs,
These who have betrayed us nicely while we took them to our rooms.

"W. H. Auden." Excerpted, with the author's consent, from *The Romantic Survival: A Study in Poetic Evolution* (London: Constable & Co., Ltd., 1957) by John Bayley, pp. 129-58.

Newman, Ciddy, Plato, Fronny, Pascal, Bowdler, Baudelaire,
Doctor Frommer, Mrs. Allan, Freud, the Baron, and Flaubert,

Lured with their compelling logic, charmed with beauty of their verse,
With their loaded sideboards whispered, "Better join us, life is worse." . . .

On the sopping esplanade or from our dingy lodgings we
Stare out dully at the rain which falls for miles into the sea.

[*Poems,* 1930. No. 22]

The gusto and sense of enjoyment here is extraordinary. As in Yeats, violence and calamity are on the way: the signs of their coming—industrial chaos, bourgeois artiness and escapism, cramped and wasted lives—are graphically described, with a pungency and detail of which Auden is already a complete master in his first 1930 volume. He has taken the metre of *Locksley Hall,* the use of which for full-blooded egotistic declamation was one of Tennyson's greatest discoveries, and he handles it with characteristic skill. He shares with Yeats an enjoyment of the situation and of the possibilities of making it *stylish.* The picture of desolation gives the reader a thrill of gratified excitement: he seems to be sharing in a vicarious *Schadenfreude,* and indulging too in the thoughtless pleasures of youth, like dropping the stone down the old working and waiting for the splash. Even the esplanade, and the hilarious precision of *sopping* and *dingy,* only give the reader that retrospective warmth which comes from remembering the boredom and glamour of childhood holidays. Staring out dully at the rain evokes at once all the rich futility of nostalgic recollection. Everything is hopeless and the country is going to the dogs, but to think this, while staring out at the rain, is somehow no inconsiderable pleasure. The attitude gives us, in some obscure way, a sense of mastery. "Man has the refuge of his gaiety." Or the refuge, at least, of a purely personal reaction. The tradition goes back much further. There is the silence of Don Juan in hell which Baudelaire admired—

Mais le calme héros, courbé sur sa rapière,
Regardait le sillage et ne daignait rien voir.

—in turn itself perhaps an echo of the more famous silence of Ajax in the *Odyssey.* What is common to all these cases is the interest of the poet and his readers in the human attitude, the sense of dramatic behaviour which human beings display in moments of crisis, disaster, or impending fear. And these attitudes are always instinctive and individual, not schooled by any intellectual process or by theories of what should be done.

Auden's variation upon this theme is to make this gesture frankly adolescent (some critics might argue that the tradition is in any case an adolescent one), and to centre the imagery and emotion of his poem in childhood experience. So far from being a call to arms, an assertion that we must get away from all this and acquire a new national identity and a new morale, the poem—as a *poem*—revels unashamedly in what we are and what we have.

> There's great delight in what we have.
> The rattle of pebbles on the shore
> Under the retreating wave.

Yeats is again an illuminating parallel. A child sees the images of disaster sharply and vividly, but irresponsibly; he does not seek to order or to understand the mess but simply adopts it as a private world, a world which gives satisfaction to his appetite and curiosity. A child might understand the silence of Ajax in hell, or rather respond in some intuitive way to its meaning, but he would not understand the causes of the Depression, the need for the elimination of the demoralised rentier class and for a change of heart that would produce a new idealism and a new dynamism in industrial relations, etc. The apparent *raison d'être* of the poem is thus in complete opposition to its effective world, "the view from Birmingham to Wolverhampton," the private world of detailed nostalgia which haunts all Auden's earlier poetry.

These points become clearer if we compare Auden's evocations of dead nightmare landscapes and approaching doom with those of T. S. Eliot in *The Rock* and in *Burnt Norton*.

> Men and bits of paper, whirled by the cold wind
> That blows before and after time,
> Wind in and out of unwholesome lungs
> Time before and time after.
> Eructation of unhealthy souls
> Into the faded air, the torpid
> Driven on the wind that sweeps the gloomy hills of London,
> Hampstead and Clerkenwell, Campden and Putney,
> Highgate, Primrose, and Ludgate. Not here
> Not here the darkness, in this twittering world.
>
> [*Burnt Norton*]

Here the nightmare is a real one, and the images, related if not to a central philosophy at least to a central *tone* of thought, are subordinate and obedient—they do not fight against the overt intention of the poem in the obstreperous delight of being themselves. The note is grave, prophetic, full of distaste; and the absence of vitality is accompanied by a curious absence of originality—the Old Testament and Blake's prophetic books, particularly the first section of Jerusalem, are visible adjuncts to the traditional mode of writing which Eliot employs. By contrast, and in spite of the metrical debt to Tennyson, Auden's poem makes a brilliantly and strikingly individual impact. But it has the vision of a child, at once neutral and passionate, while Eliot's poem has the controlled, fatigued, but "engaged" outlook of the middle-aged man. Nor is the difference simply one of the poet's age at the time the poem is written.

The dispossessed imagination may suffer from the lack of an intellectual tradition to set in order the experiences which impinge upon it. The adolescent imagination does not so suffer, because it is not called upon to judge what it experiences by any other standard than its own intensity. Hence the success, in a Romantic period, of the youthful talent, like that of Shelley or Keats: at a later date the boy prodigy becomes even more exaggeratedly youthful—a Rimbaud or a Raymond Radiguet. These were talents who succeeded because they grew up quickly, but their success prompted the question: why grow up at all? The cult of childhood in writing, its emotions and its private symbols, is one that is still with us today in consequence. The child was of course an important figure in early Romantic theory, as Wordsworth's *Immortality Ode* shows, but his position was a symbolic one: he was not valued for himself, but by a sort of inverted Platonist process he came to seem the possessor of truths which for the adult had faded into the light of common day. Moreover his position and function were quite overt and official—Shelley can compare himself to a tired child without giving the game away. But in Auden's poetry, as in much modern literature, the adolescent note—however strong and shaping its influence—is never admitted to be such. The closest that Auden has come to such an admission is his fondness for a Nietzsche quotation—"Maturity—to recover the seriousness one had as a child at play"—and his references to poetry as a particular sort of game.

Yeats's creation of "Crazy Jane" gives us a clue to the importance of the adolescent outlook in modern poetry and in Auden's in particular. For Yeats, the fool figure, who in madness and simplicity has instinctive wisdom, has much deliberate meaning and is deliberately created; but two implications are of particular interest to us: Crazy Jane defies authority, and she is fully "human" where her betters are not. Both these characteristics emerge strongly in the early poem of Auden from which we have quoted, though in an indirect way. "Authority" is at once the industrial concerns, the wreckage of which so much fascinates the poet, and the august "boon companions" who have betrayed us and at whom we can now cock a snook (the list of them is quite indiscriminate, as well as being chattily private, and includes at least two names who either were, or were to become, heroes of Auden). The human attitude resides in the poem's effective pleasure in the monstrous corpse of industry; in the accusation at one's betters that they don't really know what Life is; and in the complex gesture of nostalgia and self-acceptance which is made in the childhood image of watching the rain fall on the sea. An apparently denunciatory poem about industry and politics in fact makes its impact in very much the same way as one of Yeats's Crazy Jane poems, and it makes it by a use—how conscious a use one cannot say—of the attitudes and images of adolescence; for in an age of ideology and mechanisation only the child remains unmechanised and human.

Naturally the word "human" is a question-begging one. Why, it may be objected, should one possible activity, like *Schadenfreude* or making a graceful or derisive gesture, be more "human" than another, like setting one's ideas in order, social planning, and worrying about the future? "Spontaneous" or what Yeats understood by "passionate" would perhaps be better words. Keats, speaking of the "instinctive attitudes" of the human creature as poetry's subject, was probably thinking of the same thing. If the word is given this sense, however, it is incredible that Yeats and Auden should frequently have been criticised for being "inhuman" in their poetry. In the case of Auden especially, such an accusation seems to imply a complete failure to appreciate his poetry and to see what it essentially is.

But there are reasons for this misunderstanding. For the whole tenor of Auden's critical pronouncements on poetry has been to imply a separation between the poet as Poet, and as a responsible social being commanded to love his neighbour and behave properly, and do what he can to establish what Auden calls The Just City. The poet can indulge in all the romantic attitudes: the man must conform to the classical moral pattern. Although this dualism would have been quite intelligible to Bacon and Plato, it has never been so abruptly stated by a poet. Auden makes the distinction again and again, until we are left wondering if his obsession with it indicates some uneasiness of conscience. Why should he stress so continually that Art is one thing and Life is another, and that nothing but bad art and wrong living will come if we try to mix the two? The romantic theory of their separation is of course already well known to us: for Poe and Housman it was a necessary and comfortable one, of advantage to both sides. Housman's citing of the unpoetic phrase from the New Testament which is none the less "the greatest discovery of the moral world," and his contention that when we say we admire poetry we are often admiring something *in* it—these are confident assertions of the romantic attitude. Auden's is more deeply considered and less confident, but in a sense no less uncompromising. He sees Art as a mirror world, complete in every detail, the only difference between it and the real world being that it does not in fact exist. In Art, as Caliban puts it in *The Sea and the Mirror,* "all the phenomena of an empirically ordinary world are given. Extended objects appear to which events happen—old men catch dreadful coughs, little girls get their arms twisted. . . . All the voluntary movements are possible—crawling through flues and old sewers, sauntering past shopfronts, tiptoeing through quicksands and mined areas, running through derelict factories and across empty plains . . . all the modes of transport are available, but any sense of direction, any knowledge of where on earth one has come from or where on earth one is going to, is completely absent."

Art is thus a frozen world, locked in a series of gestures which, though fascinating and arresting, remain necessarily disconnected with the continuity of living. Of course there is a clear sense in which this is true—what happens in a book, or on the stage or screen, may be "exactly like life," but it cannot become it. But, we feel like asking, so what? Is this premise so very important? Does it lead us anywhere? Why should it need so much reiteration? The great classical writers would not have even considered it worth saying; Dante, Goethe, and Tolstoy are not disturbed by the awareness that what they write is not Life: they are preoccupied rather with the points at which Art and Life touch and interact, with the interplay of influence and resemblance, not with the initial, if basic, dissimilarity.

Why should this dissimilarity haunt Auden so much? Perhaps because he cannot really persuade himself that the way in which he likes to write, and the subject, the *ambiance* which liberate him into writing, have much to do with the part of himself that actually lives from day to day, that has come from somewhere and is going to somewhere else. Dickens, say, never appears to have been struck by such a realisation: as a novelist he seems to have complete confidence that his day-dream world and its inhabitants are as real—perhaps more real—than the stream of facts, decisions and problems that confronted him in the daily process of living. And Sartre, to take a very different example, seems to have complete confidence in the relevance to actual life of his imaginary hero Antoine Roquentin. But Auden seems to have no such confidence in his creations. The situations that appear and recur in his poems with such vividness are of the kind which we can imagine occurring to the poet as he closes his eyes for a liberating instant between two minutes of actual living. They are glimpses of life, brilliantly concrete, but seen from the unparticipating outside, as we see the screen when sitting in the cinema. They are "the *voluntary* movements"—"sauntering past shopfronts, tiptoeing through quicksands and mined areas, running through derelict factories."

> . . . Or smoking wait till hour of food
> Leaning on chained-up gate
> At edge of wood.
>
> Cigarette end smouldering on a border
> At the first garden party of the year. . . .
>
> In strangled orchards and the silent comb
> Where dogs have worried or a bird was shot.
>
> . . . the crooked claws
> Emerging into view and groping
> For handholds on the low round coping,
> As horror clambers from the well.
>
> The smiling grimy boy at the garage
> Ran out before he blew his horn. . . .
>
> Where country curates in cold bedrooms
> Dreamed of deaneries till at daybreak
> The rector's rooks with relish described
> Their stinted station.
>
> Altogether elsewhere, vast
> Herds of reindeer move across
> Miles and miles of golden moss,
> Silently and very fast.
>
> The cat has died at Ivy Dene,
> The Crowthers' pimply son has passed Matric,
> St Neots has put up light blue curtains,
> Frankie is walking out with Winnie
> And Georgie loves himself.

Black currant bushes hide the ruined opera house where badgers are said to breed in great numbers; an old horse-tramway winds away westward

> through suave foothills crowned with stone circles . . . to the north, beyond a forest inhabited by charcoal burners one can see the Devil's Bedposts quite distinctly; to the east, the museum where for sixpence one can touch the ivory chessmen.

All these extracts have in common the fact of seeming to take place "altogether elsewhere"; though they are introduced for different reasons and in different tones—ironic, lyrical, allegoric—they all exist startlingly clear of their contexts. Their resemblance to film technique, and in particular to the film close-up, is obvious (the cigarette-end smouldering in the border, the "frozen buzzard flipped over weir")—Auden has worked in films and shares with Christopher Isherwood an interest in their technique of style and build-up. Isherwood tells in *Lions and Shadows,* an autobiographical story into which Auden enters, how he would go again and again to bad films simply to observe how characters walked across a room, lit a cigarette or waited at a bus-stop. This interest in the stylisation of "humanness" is not of course unrelated to the poem's theme, just as it is not unrelated in the film, even though one may suspect that in both it takes its origin from the child's unreflective and wholehearted anthropomorphism of everything that comes into its orbit. The objects in the child's world are associated either with safety and calm or with terror and fascination—a fearful joy: and the two lie side by side. Tennyson's "dreadful hollow behind the little wood" is as necessary to the child's intense perception of its environment as Auden's "patriarchs wiser than Abraham who mended their nets on the modest wharf." As necessary, and yet as disconnected with any rational sense of the place in a total scheme of things of dreadful hollows and fishermen patriarchs. As the quotation shows (and Auden has commented on Tennyson's infantile approach to poetry with the knowingness of the man who recognises his obsession commenting on the man who doesn't), Tennyson felt the effectiveness of "fearful joy" in securing the poetic assent of the reader. Auden recognises it much more consciously; makes use of it, makes fun of it, analyses it, distrusts it. We are separated from childhood, he hints, as we are separated from art. We can never get back there and it is disastrous to try. The moods appropriate to childhood and to poetry cannot be permitted free play in a grown-up world and a responsible society. "All poets," he says in an essay, "adore explosions, thunderstorms, tornadoes, conflagrations, ruins, scenes of spectacular carnage. The poetical imagination is therefore not at all a desirable quality in a chief of state." All poets with the particular romantic bent of Auden, one might qualify, and such a poet also adores private languages, schoolboy symbols, sinister landscapes in which hikers and waiters are really spies and agents of the Adversary or "They," and "amusing ourselves on what would otherwise have been a very dull evening indeed by planning to seize the post office across the river."

And so, as he says in another essay, "there must always be two kinds of art—escape art, for man needs escape as he needs food and deep sleep, and parable art, that art which shall teach man to unlearn hatred and learn love." The dichotomy so stated seems one of almost staggering crudity. Is there indeed no middle way between the "altogether elsewhere" where "the minotaur of authority is just a roly-poly ruminant and nothing is at stake," and art which is consciously connected with some ethical scheme for our betterment? Not for the poet, would seem to be Auden's reply, and indeed in his own poetic development and practice the dichotomy is very marked: his critical bluntness seems to arise from the *fait accompli* of his own work and its individual quality. Perhaps for the novelist though: Auden has always venerated this form of art, in which the phenomenology of life can be seen steadily and commented on *in extenso*. "A higher art than poetry altogether," he calls it in one of his *Letters to Lord Byron,* and in his sonnet *The Novelist* he says that the poet, "encased in talent like a uniform," can dash forward like a hussar or amaze us like a thunderstorm, but cannot, he implies, do very much else. The suggestion of talent—perhaps the gift of conveying the delight of a private world or a private game—as an *insulator,* is as revealing as the thunderstorm image: Auden has already told us that the poet adores such displays. But it is different for the novelist.

> For, to achieve his lightest wish, he must
> Become the whole of boredom, subject to
> Vulgar complaints like love, among the Just
>
> Be just, among the Filthy filthy too,
> And in his own weak person, if he can,
> Must suffer dully all the wrongs of Man.

This deprecation of poetry—"the old innocent game of playing God with words"—is not a defensive or obscurantist attitude in Auden: he does not imply, as Romantics like Housman did—that poetry is a pure mystery to be kept separate from the vulgar hurly-burly of affairs. Nor is it like music, of which Auden observes

> Only your notes are pure contraption,
> Only your song is an absolute gift.

Music, like Housman's poetry, may "cascade"—in Auden's enchanting phrase—"the falls of the knee and the weirs of the spine," but poetry is rather different, not pure contraption but robust game. None the less,

> The gulf between frivolity and seriousness, between choosing to obey the rules of a game which it does not matter whether you play or not, and choosing to obey the rules of life which you have to live whether you like it or not, and where the rules are necessary because they do not cease to exist if you disobey them but operate within you to your own destruction —this gulf is so infinite that all talk about children's games being a preparation for adult life is misleading twaddle.
>
> [*Squares and Oblongs*]

The game is not a preparation for adult life; the attitudes of poetry are not valid in living. Again we feel inclined to retort: "But you are thinking of your own poetry, or of poetry that in some way resembles it." Is Auden taking this Platonic line because Romantic poetry, *if taken seriously* and allowed to influence our attitudes to life, may encourage vicious attitudes, and put itself, as T. S. Eliot might say, at the service of unacceptable ideas? Certainly it is possible to imagine the poetry of Shelley, say (which Auden detests), or that of Housman or Yeats, exercising a temporary influence over the behaviour of the young which could be called a bad influence. Suicides may have followed from a perusal of the *Shropshire Lad*. In Japan, where translations of Housman are popular, they no doubt have. Yeats's aesthetic attitude might be said to regard life as a game—"a test of inborn *aretē*" as Auden says about the Greek attitude to life—and such an *aretē* of stylish toughness rather than stylish sensitivity might appeal to would-be aesthetes who had begun to find Pater rather old-fashioned. But this point is clearly a minor one: as soon as one considers specific instances, the question of whether poetry is or is not capable of "doing harm" becomes quite unreal. Whether or not one finds significance in Auden's view of poetry as a voluntary game and life as an involuntary task, one finds no difficulty in agreeing that poetry is not ideology. It is far too complete, the formal, pattern, or "game" aspect of it is much too important, for its "ideas" to have free play. Auden despises Shelley for having called poets "the unacknowledged legislators of the world" and says that such a description fits the secret police better. Or, one might add, the great ideologues. The ideas of Rousseau, Nietzsche, and Marx have had a much more obvious and drastic effect on human behaviour than the poetry of either Shelley or Shakespeare.

None the less, Auden is surely wrong in maintaining that because of the "gratuitous" nature of poetry it has nothing to teach us about life and can only do harm if it tries. The potential harm consists in treating the writing—and presumably the reading—of poetry "as if it were a kind of religious technique, a way of learning to be happy and good." The distinction is surely too simple. If poetry is not religion must it therefore be a game? Even if it is, why the existential sternness of this complete divorce between games and life?—the latter is for most people a sufficiently complex affair to include the former. Manners, customs, all the sane ceremonial of living, could easily be called a game according to Auden's definition: yet they occupy an important place in life, and poetry as a part of them surely deserves to be considered, to use an old-fashioned phrase, as a civilising influence?

In another context, and with the inconsistency which is such an endearing feature of Yeats's critical attitudes, Auden virtually admits this. He writes in the notes to the *New Year Letter:*

> Wagner is perhaps the greatest genius that ever lived. But in the expression of suffering only. Happiness, social life, mystical joy, success, were completely beyond him. For spontaneous happiness, friendship, requited love, we must go elsewhere—to Mozart.
>
> For the strong, the intelligent, the healthy, the successful, those on whom, just because they are so, falls the duty of understanding weakness, stupidity, disease and failure in order that they may cure them, Wagner's operas are essential, a constant source of delight. They *must* listen to him.
>
> But who should never be allowed to listen to Wagner? The unhappy, the disappointed, the politically ambitious, the self-pitying, those who imagine themselves misunderstood, the Wagnerians. And to whom should they be compelled to listen?—to Mozart and Beethoven.

What has happened to music as pure contraption, as absolute gift? And Mozart emerges as the musician of social graces and games, of civilised and happy living, who is therapeutic in effect for precisely this reason. Art takes on the nature not of a game but of occupational therapy. We can imagine the neurotic being submitted to a course not of Mozart only, but of Ariosto, Gay, Calverley, and the *Oxford Book of Light Verse*. The civilising influence becomes a compulsory routine, while Auden seems to regard with equanimity the idea that we might be conditioned to benefit from art which makes no instinctive appeal to our temperament.

Although they may at times be inconsistent, all Auden's ideas about art and poetry are extremely forthright; there are no hesitations or qualifications, and as we have seen from the contrast he draws between "escape art" and "parable art" he is never afraid of being graphic, even crude.

The violence of his contrasts comes from his dependence on two sources of theory: first, Freud, and second, Kierkegaard and the Existentialists—the influence of the second increasing as that of the first has waned. Freud saw art as a substitute for power where the artist was concerned, a substitute in fantasy for what the artist's disposition denied him in life—"power, honour, riches, and the love of women." And though there is for the artist "a path back to reality" it lies in revealing for his public "the comfort and consolation of their own unconscious sources of pleasure," and hence winning in fact by his reputation the rewards that life had previously denied him. Art, moreover, "seldom dares to make any attack on the realm of reality." Auden in his earlier work accepts and makes frequent references to Freud's point of view. Michael Ransom in *The Ascent of F.6* censures Dante in typically Freudian terms.

> It was not Virtue those lips, which involuntary privation had made so bitter, could pray for; it was not Knowledge; it was Power. Power to exact for every snub, every headache, every unfallen beauty, an absolute revenge; wit with a stroke of the pen to make a neighbour's vineyard a lake of fire and to create in his private desert the austere music of the angels or the happy extravagance of a fair.

In a later essay Auden has added a significant gloss to this:

> In primitive societies the incantation of a curse is believed to be practically as effective as a stab with a knife, but aesthetics only begins when it is realised that one man curses another because he knows that he is unable to murder him.
>
> [*Mimesis and Allegory*]

"*Because* he knows"—Auden's conviction of the sharply self-conscious processes in the author's mind is certainly applicable to himself. No poet perhaps has ever been more determined to be conscious of what he is doing and his reasons for doing it. And with Auden there is no gap between the creator and the commentator, although there is frequently a marked differentiation in *effect* between the joyous pursuit of a phrase or image for its own sake and the part that it is intended to play in the reasoned dimension of the poem. When he writes, for example, of the "collarless herds who eat blancmange and have never said anything witty," the charm of the phrase is in the sheer unfairness and irresponsibility of its gusto and wit. He is speaking of the Others, the dim creatures, the masses outside the exclusive sparkle of the gang. He cannot harm them by speaking of them in this way—his own theory protects him there—and, conversely, a kind of malice which must never be allowed in life is finding in art a graceful and easy outlet. That is why, as Auden reiterates again and again,

> . . . these halcyon structures are useful
> As structures go—though not to be confused
> With anything really important
> Like feeding strays or looking pleased when caught
> By a bore or a hideola.
>
> [*Music is International*]

"Be nice in life and in poetry you can be as nasty as you please"—the advice seems too clear-cut, too sanitative, too chilling, a kind of poetic *Ketman* which forbids life and literature to meet and mingle in the passionate and unself-conscious manner they once did.

And it has its practical disadvantages for the artist. It means we find it almost impossible to take him seriously. We can laugh at or with him; admire his technical brilliance and the virtuosity of his language; shudder delightfully at the images in which he embodies his private nightmares and connect them with those Freudian "unconscious sources" of our own. But is this enough? Not only is Auden always intensely conscious of what he is doing: he makes us, his readers, equally conscious of what is happening to us, and how, and why. His clinical attitude prohibits the nebulous, the profundity which moves us but which we cannot quite grasp. Perhaps because, as he says,

> What we find rousing or touching
> Tells us little and confuses us much. . . .

and confusion is a dangerous frame of mind, leading to abuses and difficulties in the sphere of life. Auden does not seem to admit the existence of a Keatsian "negative capability" in poetry, a state of fruitful uncertainty, of being on the edge of some truth whose centre we cannot from its very nature express. Only in one or two of his earliest poems—Numbers 18 and 19 in *Poems* 1930 for instance—does he seem to be poetically "in the dark" and groping towards something which he cannot apprehend with precision.

He shares with T. S. Eliot this enormous self-consciousness—it is one of the few points which they have in common. In Eliot it takes the form of a deprecation, an honest enquiry, an implied refusal to posture before the reader and dazzle him with a display of poetical virtuosity.

That was a way of putting it—not very satisfactory,
A periphrastic study in a worn-out poetical fashion
Leaving one still with the intolerable wrestle
With words and meanings. The poetry does not matter.
[*East Coker*]

Following a passage that is, as it were, wearily rhetorical and artificial ("What is the late November doing"), this disclaimer may baffle and irritate the reader, but it certainly leaves him in no doubt about the poet's honesty. It is almost a device for creating an atmosphere of sincerity. In Auden's case the fact that "the poetry does not matter" is rather differently conveyed: the poet does not attempt to disguise the fact that he is a virtuoso whose job it is to give a good performance, but his gestures as he does so are ironical, and the irony is often directed at the poet himself. In both cases the idea that the poetry is important is not entertained, but whereas for Eliot the poetry is part of a general ethos which is of the very first importance, for Auden it is not. This is perhaps why we can take Eliot seriously even when he is being his most exasperatingly deprecating and self-conscious, whereas the Auden irony and urbanity we follow gladly for their own sake and can only be persuaded of their final seriousness by external means, i.e. by the subject matter—refugees, war, etc.—which the poet puts before us. Auden has always shown a great interest in light verse and the ironic approach, and we must return for a fuller examination of his methods here, but our point for the moment is the connection between such an approach and the contemporary poetic self-consciousness. Deprecation in Eliot, irony in Auden, are symptoms of the same condition.

Because of his brisk desire to make distinctions between life and art, escape and parable, the localising effects of this self-consciousness are much more apparent in Auden than in Eliot. Consider an image of Auden's which has been quoted before. It occurs in the *New Year Letter,* where Auden is illustrating the theological concept that Man's life is a state of Becoming, not of Being, and that though accidental "spots of time" may occur in which he can sample the perfection of Being he must not try to stay in this condition or prolong it, or else

The sky grows crimson with a curse
The flowers change colour for the worse,
He hears behind his back the wicket
Padlock itself, from the dark thicket
The chuckle with no healthy cause,

And, helpless, sees the crooked claws
Emerging into view and groping
For hand-holds on the low round coping,
As Horror clambers from the well:
For he has sprung the trap of Hell.
[*New Year Letter*]

The image is delightful, but it is pure M. R. James. Its associations for the reader are of a quite different kind from those explanatory concepts of Being and Becoming which Auden with his usual virtuosity deploys. Whatever we feel when we try to prolong the moment "at the still point of the turning world," as Eliot calls it, it would surely not be this: the world where such *frissons* of cheerful horror occur is all too obviously the normal day-to-day world. The images of possession and loss in which Eliot, on the other hand, describes a similar order of experience in the *Four Quartets* does seem to coincide at a deep level with what we may ourselves have felt about such experience.

Then a cloud passed, and the pool was empty.
[*Burnt Norton*]

Dawn points, and another day
Prepares for heat and silence. Out at sea the dawn wind
Wrinkles and slides.
[*East Coker*]

"No artist," writes Auden, "not even Eliot, can prevent his work being used as magic, for that is what all of us, highbrow and lowbrow alike, secretly want Art to be." And it is a guilty secret.

Shame at our shortcomings makes
Lame magicians of us all,
Forcing our invention to
An illegal miracle
And a theatre of disguise. . . .
[*Epithalamion*]

The shame of Magic is that it solves easily what in life can only be solved partially and with continual effort. And this consciousness of the possibility of poetry being used as an incantation, as a quick way to a satisfaction of the feelings, haunts Auden, perhaps because the "magical" power of his own poetry is so obvious and so impressive. But it is a quick self-contained "magical" satisfaction that the Auden quotation, divorced from its context, gives us, and though the poet is careful to dissipate such impressions as much as he can by descent into irony—"wit that spoils Romantic art," as he calls it—or into flat statement or exhortation, it is the "magical" passages that remain with the reader. Irony does not necessarily destroy magic, for, as we shall see later, it may itself be one of magic's expedients. What does destroy it is Eliot's deliberate and weary refusal to keep up the incantation: by shrugging his shoulders with a "that was a way of putting it" he effectively checks any attempt of the reader to repose in an insulated enjoyment of the passage. And at what a cost! If this is a preventive against magic, we should have good grounds for preferring magic instead. Whether true or not, Auden's admission that magic is what we want poetry to be gives the clue to the real source of vitality in his own poetry.

None the less, Auden's attitude implies a certain desperation. How can "magic" and parable ever be reconciled by a poet who is so obsessed with the difference between them? How can our reaction be anything but ambiguous towards a poetry that is by implication telling us: "I may read like a charm but you must not take me for one. My subject is Love, the Just City, right conduct, the nature of moral and religious choice, etc." Dante's subject was not dissimilar—the nature of the universe, of the highest wisdom and divine love—but we cannot imagine Dante concerned about the way in which this might be mistaken for, or taken as, an autotelic charm, a surrogate power and glory. It might be argued that many, if not most, of Dante's readers today do in fact take it as such, and that Auden is only being realistic in admitting this, but there is all the difference between a poetry that is not composed in the expectation that the reader will rest upon its qualities in a kind of aesthetic full-stop, finding in them "the consolation of his own unconscious sources of pleasure," and a poetry which secretly admits that this will probably happen.

Nor is the rigour of the dichotomy apparently lessened by existentialist theories of art. "One must get out of the poetical into the existential" is one of Auden's favourite Kierkegaard quotations; another, "the poet's sin is to poeticise instead of being." And by implication it is his reader's sin to read the poetry instead of living. In Kierkegaard the Aesthetic and the Ethical are sharply divided—two stages from one to the other of which the individual must move. And Sartre is similarly emphatic. "The real is never beautiful," he writes. "Beauty is a value which can apply only to the imaginary, and whose essential structure involves the nullification of the world. This is why it is foolish to confuse ethics and aesthetics. The values of the Good presuppose being-in-the-world; they are concerned with behaviour in real contexts and are subject from the start to the essential absurdity of existence." The debt of Auden's critical outlook to pronouncements of this type is obvious, and it is this bleak critical climate which is accepted in the context of his poems. And not only accepted, but exploited sometimes with a positive buoyancy. Auden delights in turning into poetry—in "nullifying" into the poetic as Sartre might call it—the most ragged and "viscous" aspects and experiences of life. He seems to find its randomness and existential absurdity a challenge to his skill. *The Age of Anxiety* is particularly full of such passages.

In a vacant lot
We built a bonfire and burned alive
Some stolen tyres. How strong and good one
Felt at first, how fagged coming home through
The urban evening. Heavy like us
Sank the gas-tanks—it was supper time.
In hot houses helpless babies and
Telephones gabbled untidy cries,
And on embankments black with burnt grass
Shambling freight-trains were shunted away
Past crimson clouds.

The brilliancy of description ends there. It does not lead anywhere—(indeed it is difficult to see where anything in *The Age of Anxiety* can be said to lead)—but it conveys a sense of the occasion at once and with vivid accuracy, and gives the reader the unpursuing satisfaction of contemplating a formal triumph. It is difficult for the most conscientious reader—if he enjoys the passage at all—not to repose upon the event described, upon its sense of the particular and upon the flavour of nostalgic recollection which it holds. A comparison with Eliot is again legitimate and illuminating. *Preludes* are equally careful evocations of the shabby and incomplete urban moment.

The burnt-out ends of smoky days
And now a gusty shower wraps
The grimy scraps
Of withered leaves about your feet
And newspapers from vacant lots;
The showers beat
On broken blinds and chimney-pots. . . .

But the poet not only has a general and "ethical" comment to make on this world ("the notion of some infinitely gentle, infinitely suffering thing")—he is also eager to put us in touch with his own *feelings* about the thing described and hence to induce a corresponding feeling, perhaps of depression or indignation, in us, which will lead us away from aesthetic satisfaction and back to the emotions of daily life. This is not the case in Auden. Magic persists, with the tacit encouragement of the author, who "cannot prevent" his work being used in this way.

Expert in self-diagnosis, Auden has even indicated how the "unromantic" and satirical approach can itself lead to the state of aesthetic equilibrium and completeness which constitutes Magic. The more perceptive and unified the approach, the greater the chance that the intelligent reader will simply sit back and enjoy the situation, will enjoy particularly the dazzling *mots* and turns of phrase that mock at him for so enjoying it! As Caliban puts it in *The Sea and the Mirror:*

> In representing to you your condition of estrangement from the truth, [the poet] is doomed to fail the more he succeeds, for the more truthfully he paints the condition, the less clearly can he indicate the truth from which it is estranged, and, worse still, the more sharply he defines the estrangement itself—and, ultimately, what other aim and justification has he, what else exactly *is* the artistic gift which he is forbidden to hide, if not to make you unforgettably conscious of the ungarnished offended gap between what you so questionably are and what you are commanded without any question to become, of the unqualified No that opposes your every step in any direction?—the more he must strengthen your delusion that an awareness of the gap is itself a bridge, your interest in your imprisonment a release, so that, far from your being led by him to contrition and surrender, your dialogue, using his words, with yourself about yourself, becomes the one activity which never, like devouring or collecting or spending, lets you down, the one game which can be guaranteed, whatever the company, to catch on. . . .

With this penetrating piece of defeatism, Auden voices his own doubts about his poetry. Of what use is the most biting irony, the most urgent moral tone, if they are to be regarded as just two more delightful tricks in the craftsman's range? We agree, but we cannot help feeling that this very perspicacity shows the problem to be a little unreal—unreal, that is, to those who cannot see it so clearly because they are not accustomed to think of poetry as a subtle game of self-conscious nuances between poet and reader. If we take the T. S. Eliot quotation just referred to, are we conscious after reading it of the issue which Caliban puts with such Jamesian elaboration? If the poetry and the poet's feelings move us, then they move us, and not in so different a way from the manner in which the actual experiences described might have done. The poet's "notion" is not so different from the one which we might have had: that, at any rate, is our feeling if we have enjoyed and admired the poem, and we should have a similar impression after reading a poem of Wordsworth or many others.

But with Auden we do not. Where his poetry is concerned Caliban's case has real cogency, for he does appear as the poet of a highly self-conscious private conspiracy between poet and reader, and no one is more conscious of this than Auden himself. But "awareness of a gap is not a bridge," and the poet must endure this self-consciousness just as the reader, if he is fully to appreciate the poetry, must understand it. Critics of Auden have always appeared to find it difficult to talk about his poetry, as opposed to the borrowed materials in it, and its nominal pre-occupations: it is this that makes even a serious and informed critical approach seem so curiously beside the point. Thus Richard Hoggart often writes in his excellent study of the poet in a manner which would seriously mislead an uninformed but intelligent poetry reader—say a foreigner—about what the *actual* virtues of Auden's poetry are.

> Auden combines an intense interest in the human heart with a desire to reform society, and he thinks our psychological ills greater than our political. . . . He is convinced of the urgent need for mental therapy; he believes that the spread and assimilation of the findings of psychology can help society towards health; he is sure that such action is morally desirable; he thinks it is owed to "the human creature we must nurse to sense and decency."

Accurate and unimpeachable statements. But how little relationship they bear to the reality of the verse! If, on the other hand, one were to write of T. S. Eliot's poetry like this, and for the same kind of reader, there would be no such gap. "Eliot combines a strong interest in tradition and the Church and their possible place in modern society with a more personal preoccupation with the sources of peace and virtue for the individual in the understanding of time." Such introductory remarks, though banal, would not be misleading, nor would the enquirer after reading them be startled by what he found in Eliot. One might sum up the matter by saying that while all Auden's apparently public, outgoing themes are in fact private and self-contained, Eliot's, even at their most exploratory and personal, retain a public susceptibility to exegesis and the straightforward explanatory gloss. To stress the inclusive and journalistic aspects of Auden's talent is in a sense as remote from his poetry as it would be to enumerate Mallarmé's subjects or Poe's attitudes to life and society.

I do not mean by this that Auden writes "pure" poetry or anything approximating to it. But such poetry is undoubtedly a part of what he means by Magic, though in his case it is not the recherché affair of the Symbolists, but a distillation of his widespread interests and his fascination with place and people. Auden has followed Yeats in showing how the intense private world of symbolism can be brought right out into the open, eclecticised, and pegged down to every point of contemporary interest and everyday life, while remaining none the less in a private and even a substitute world. Auden is an emancipator of Romantic Symbolism, but it is in this tradition that his roots lie, and it is by the criteria applied to such poetry that he should ultimately be judged. Attacks on Auden are invariably based on his irresponsibility, has unfounded pretensions to intellectual power and weight, and his enjoyment of the private joke or absurdity for its own sake, etc., and all these strictures lose their force if his poetry is read for what it is, and not for what his critics—misled by the poet's ambiguous attitude—have supposed it is attempting to be.

Auden's is not public poetry in the sense in which Eliot's—even at its most meditative—can be said to be. But as we have seen, both poets share the extreme critical self-consciousness common among writers today, and it is for this reason that both can best be approached via their critical pronouncements and their attitude to poetry. We have examined some of the implications of Auden's criticism and applied it to his work in general. We must now make a more detailed survey of his poetic development as it is revealed in individual poems.

What makes a poem of Auden good or bad? The question, baldly put, can be as baldly answered: whether or not it is filled with vivid personal apprehensions of things—things and people, but above all things, for though Auden never regards people wantonly or inhumanly he does depersonalise them and transform them into a bizarre extension of object or place. Their significance to the poet as emblems of some general condition may be large, but they are always seen against some appropriate background or linked to their unique and revealing properties of clothing, accent, or facial tic. Auden is a Symbolist of the common fate, the humdrum situation. As soon as he generalises, steps out of the heightened world of the Symbolist's still life, his poetry sags and loses momentum. He speaks in the *New Year Letter* of "Rilke whom Der Dinge bless, the Santa Claus of loneliness," and just as Rilke was preoccupied in his poetry with *things* and their place in space, the space in which "flowers endlessly prolong themselves," so Auden is absorbed in the spectacle of things and people in their medium of isolation. There are reasons for this medium—historical, social, or psychological—and these the poet sets himself to express with confidence and knowledge, but it is the vision itself that counts, and the fact that the poet has selected it, rather than that he can go on to give reasons for his selection.

It is a very English vision, as English as that of Dickens. Though clinical, it is also extremely parochial. And the ideal Auden reader should also have Dickensian tastes: he should be not unlike George Eliot's Mrs Linnet. Mrs Linnet was fond of reading the biographies of celebrated preachers, "and wherever there was a predominance of Zion and the River of Life, she turned to the next page; but any passage in which she saw such promising nouns as 'smallpox,' 'pony,' or 'boots and shoes,' at once arrested her." As a preacher, even though he rarely adopts in fact the "loose immodest tone" of which he—with characteristic self-awareness—accuses himself, Auden can only expect to suffer the fate of Mrs Linnet's favourite divines. Any successful "parable art" which he accomplishes is done through the medium of the boots and shoes, the pony and the smallpox, as it were, and this is very nearly equivalent to saying that Mallarmé's "preaching" must be done through his swans and fauns and white pages, or Yeats's through Byzantium and the Gyres and the "half-legendary" Irishmen of his imagination. Auden's mythology is as effective and magical as theirs, and as able to suggest dimensions of meaning in which the rationalising mind has little place.

The Career of W. H. Auden

by G. S. Fraser

I. *Auden as the Young Prophet*

The Orators, an English Study came out in 1932, when its author, Mr. W. H. Auden, was in his twenty-sixth year. It was his second important book (the first was the *Poems* of 1930). He thinks it, now, a failure. Judging very stringently, he is right, but I wish there were a poet of twenty-five who was likely to give us in the late 1950s a failure equally exciting. The great and notable quality of the language, prose and verse, throughout *The Orators,* is punch, impact, vigour. The verse can be as striking as this: the speaker, one should explain, is a beggar, one of the dispossessed of the classical world, feeling that "the barbarians may be some sort of solution": he is also one of the dispossessed of liberal, and growingly Fascist, Europe in the 1930s, looking wistfully towards a symbolic Russia:

> "Won't you speak louder?
> Have you heard of someone swifter than Syrian horses?
> Has he thrown the bully of Corinth in the sanded circle?
> Has he crossed the Isthmus already? Is he seeking brilliant
> Athens and us?"

The prose can be as pungently concentrated as this, an image of the human spirit crucified by excessive self-love:

> "With odd dark eyes like windows, a lair for engines, they pass suffering more and more from cataract or deafness, leaving behind them diaries full of incomprehensible jottings, complaints less heard than the creaking of a wind pump on a moor."

"The Career of W. H. Auden" (Editor's title). From *Vision and Rhetoric: Studies in Modern Poetry* (London: Faber & Faber, Ltd., 1959) by G. S. Fraser, pp. 149-78.

The book, of course, contains other passages that have worn less well. In the six odes at the end, in particular, there is too much of that scout-masterish breeziness, the one aspect of Mr. Auden's complex poetic personality which I have never been able to stand:

> Queer to these birds; yes, very queer,
> But to the tryers such a dear,
> Only hard
> On smuggling, smartness, and self regard. . . .

Whether this is Dr. Arnold as God, or God as Dr. Arnold, it is equally hard to take. What may also annoy readers now, though it was very stimulating in 1932, is the insolently ostentatious privacy of many of the references:

> Of all the healers, granny in mittens, the Mop,
> the white surgeon,
> And loony Layard.

Mr. Layard, I discovered recently, is a Jungian psychologist who may have been the first to introduce the young Auden to Groddeck. Who or what "the Mop" was must remain a mystery till some thesis-manufacturer bothers to write to Mr. Auden and ask. But to a young reader in the early 1930s, these incidental obscurities did not seem to matter so much. The general drift seemed so clear.

Was it, though? If you had asked me what *The Orators* was "about," twenty-four years ago, when I was an undergraduate, I should have said it was about the decay of English energy and the need to renew that energy through insight and action; and that the action was envisaged, in the book, mainly as that of small groups—discontented sons of the ruling classes—of dedicated young men. That would have been correct, up to a point. But the interesting thing is this. In the 1930s, I took it for granted, as everyone did (and as Auden, with his description of himself as a "pink liberal" probably at a surface level also took for granted), that the implied politics were more or less Marxist. They seem to me now the politics of a romantic radical of the Right. What the airman, in the prose section which is the moral core of the book, *Journal of an Airman,* dreams of is the renewed simplicity of a patriarchal order:

> The man shall love the work; the woman shall receive him as the divine representative; the child shall be born as the sign of the trust; the friend shall laugh at the joke apparently obscure.

Or, in the verse, even more strikingly:

> All of the women and most of the men
> Shall work with their hands and not think again. . . .

These are not liberal or democratic sentiments. Manual therapy may be as good for a sick society as for a sick individual, but all the same these are the sentiments of idealistic Fascism. "All of the women . . . ," also, does take one aback. And the bias behind the phrase is a recurrent one: "There is something peculiarly horrible about the idea of women pilots," and " 'What a wonderful woman she is!' Not so fast. Wait till you see her son."

The airman of the *Journal* feels, in fact, that what is valuable in his heritage comes from men. The dead Uncle, who initiated him into the meaning of life, is spiritually more truly his "ancestor" than his uncomprehending mother is. Auden works out this idea, with a diagram, in rather boring detail. But it is a key idea: one negative way of describing the atmosphere of his work throughout the 1930s is to say that the image of the Muse is absent except in the sinister transformed shape of the "terrible Mother." A mother-landscape image is sinisterly transformed in the prologue to *The Orators* itself. When the Hero returns from completing his task, the Muse who should welcome him has become (because he has subtly betrayed her) an ogress:

> And yet this prophet, homing the day is ended,
> Receives odd welcome from the country he so defended:
> The band roars "Coward, Coward," in his fever,
> The giantess shuffles nearer, cries, "Deceiver."

For the poets of the 1930s, in fact, the Hero has ceased to be the Muse's lover, he has become her competitor. Similarly it was not the female image of Nature ("By landscape reminded once of his mother's figure") that interested them so much as the male use of nature, the ruined powerhouses, the hangars, the pylons.

So, if I were asked now what I thought *The Orators* is "about," I should say something like this. It is about romantic male solidarity, about the idea of being initiated into the group of young braves of the tribe. Or, to take another image, it is about knightliness ("airman" equals "cavalier"). In England, the ordinary working-class or lower-middle-class young man gets such an initiation into an all-male society only when there is a World War. The upper middle classes and the aristocracy get it all the time from the public-school tradition, from compulsory games, for instance, the prefect system, and the O.T.C. Baden-Powell tried to give it to everybody, or to a much wider section of the population, through the Boy Scouts. These are the reasons why the first book of *The Orators* is called "The Initiates," why it begins with a parody of a school prize-giving speech, and why in the odes one is sometimes reminded (not so incongruously as might at first appear) of Kipling or Newbolt:

> Time to change guard:
> Boy, the quarrel was before your time, the aggressor
> No one you know.

Moreover, *The Orators* is not only about romantic male solidarity in general; more particularly, it is about the fantasies of power and the daydreams of violent social change which this solidarity can evoke, in periods of decay, among gifted and discontented young men. Auden is certainly imaginatively attracted, in many passages of *The Orators,* to a mood that can engender Fascism; but the great moral distinction of the book is how he steps back on his tracks. In *Journal of an Airman* he in the end undermines, with ruthless insight, his own fantasies.

That ruthless insight lies behind such a passage as this:

> In hours of gentleness always to remember my Uncle, the connection between the last desperate appeals of the lost for help scribbled on the walls of public latrines and such a letter as this.

There is a less compressed, but very moving, passage in which the "I" of the *Journal* has a long conversation with an imaginary critic who asks him what conceivable general interest an accumulation of private fantasies and allusions, a myth and an ethos derived from the shared experiences of the "small group," can have. Desperately trying to convey "the interest," all the "I" can do is to recall private jokes, give lists of names of friends, sketch out obscurely a traumatic experience. His interlocutor replies inexorably: "Yes, but the interest?" It is partly the same sort of "interest" as that of the "Mortmere" world, the world of small-group folklore, described by Isherwood in *Lions and Shadows.* To a wider audience, much of "the interest," in this sense, *must* remain incommunicable; but is the very *existence* of this "interest"—a severe critic of Mr. Auden, like Dr. Leavis, would tend to say so—merely a small group's self-flattering delusion?

The "I" of *The Journal of an Airman* moves on from such self-questionings to hysterical (though also hysterically funny) fantasies about violent revolution. He has already sketched out, with paranoiac wit, as the opposite of the "airman" with his "self-care," the many faces of the "self-regard" of the "enemy":

> Three kinds of enemy face—the June bride—
> the favourite puss—the stone in the rain.

It is the enemy's "self-regard" which introduces "inert velocities" into what would otherwise be a self-regulating system. But at the end the "I" recognizes that these are "thoughts suitable to a sanatorium." He recovers humility. He is suddenly able to relate his humiliating kleptomania, his compulsive pocketing of small objects, to the element of grossness—of self-flattery, blindness, and brutality—in his fantasies. His hands "stole to force a hearing." He realizes also (to put it more simply and flatly than Auden does) that "the enemy" is essentially a projection of his own unconscious inner aggressiveness, his will to dominate. He breaks off a relationship which he values, because he feels that God must disapprove of it. He faces calmly some ordeal he has to face (in view of the sinister "Letter to a Wound" in an earlier section, and of the many scattered references to surgery throughout *The Orators,* it may be an operation). The last entry is: "Hands in perfect order."

It is disturbing, however, in the six odes which follow *Journal of an Airman,* that Auden still often seems to be functioning at the level of the airman's fantasies rather than his insights. There is a strange effect of double focus, insight mounted on fantasy. Nothing could be more effective than some of the hard-hitting satire, rather Skeltonic in tone, on well-known iniquities of the early Thirties; but all this is set in a framework of a world that is to be made over by Rex, Christopher, Stephen, loony Layard, and the rest of "the boys"—in the framework of an inanely complacent vision of a revolution working from the top down, engineered by an *élite.* There is not really that sentimentalization of the working classes of which the poets of the 1930s are sometimes accused:

> Dyers and bakers
> And boiler-tube makers,

Poofs and ponces,
All of them dunces.
Those over thirty,
Ugly and dirty. . . .

One would say that Auden didn't trust or respect the common people enough. And to make two sharp observations: it was the "Dyers and bakers/And boiler-tube makers," not Rex or Wystan, who at El Alamein in 1942 did in fact "throw the bully of Corinth in the sanded circle"; it was the people who ought to "work on the land and not think again," not Christopher or Stephen, who brought about the profoundly important peaceful social revolution of 1945. Yet if Auden's solutions were often fantastic, his eye for the problem was unerring: "What do you think about England, this country of ours where nobody is well?" And he was right to seek the roots of that illness in misdirected and inadequate love, in the wrong use of the spirit. He was right, also, to harangue and clamour. In the sort of detailed social remedies it suggests, *The Orators* may be far off the mark as Carlyle's *Past and Present.* But like that book it stirred the consciences of intelligent young men in a bad time. That, in modern times, is what we expect a prophet to do.

II. *Auden in Midstream*

"With his unattractive stock-in-trade, and his clap-trap," says Kathleen Raine, "Auden, nevertheless, as none of the rest do, touches the human heart." The unattractive stock-in-trade is, I suspect, for Miss Raine the facile use of generalizations—the taking of a leading idea from Freud, from Marx, and now from Kierkegaard, and seeing how it works out in a different context. It is the adoption, by a powerful but not a very scrupulous intellect, of any convenient "working scheme." (The first section of *The Orators,* with its startling application of Dante's ideas about love, as the only human motive, to the problems of public-school life, is an admirable example of Auden's pragmatism at its most fruitful and illuminating level.) God, like the libido, or like the dialectic, is for Auden chiefly a useful generalization; assuming the existence of God, he finds it possible to solve certain problems. The clap-trap is the unction, the over-persuasiveness, the mixture of blarney and bullying that goes with this sort of pragmatism. Hugh Sykes Davies, an excellent critic, who writes too little, has hinted at the morally repellent side of Auden's attitudes . . . the element that has something in common even with

Buchmanism. "It is not possible," Sykes Davies says, "to adopt a new theory or a new loyalty overnight for valid reasons, and the reasons for such overnight changes are always invalid. The crisis in the patient's ideas and feelings does not arise from observation and speculation, but from internal psychological problems, of course unperceived; and the solution is determined not by observation and speculation, but by the needs of the psychological condition. . . . Every convert is psychologically ill. . . . Morally, he disgusts because the act of conversion solidifies personal neuroses into social form. *In time, converts band together in such numbers that they, the diseased, can interfere with the healthy unconverted—and they are always anxious to do this.*" It must be admitted that it is almost too easy to apply this generalization to Auden. He has, since he began, been threatening his readers with a variety of calamities—disease, madness, death in war or revolution, and now eternal damnation. He has, as he admits himself,

> Adopted what I would disown
> The preacher's loose immodest tone.

Yet, when all this is said, Auden does remain the most considerable poet of his generation. He does, as Miss Raine says, touch the human heart. He cannot be dismissed just by saying that one doesn't believe what he says, and doubts (because he is too emphatic about it) whether he really believes it himself. Auden's attitudes, reduced to average prose, would result in a writer as unpleasant as, say, Mr. Middleton Murry. But they are not reduced to average prose. They are *used* for rather extraordinary poetry.

Let us take an example of the clap-trap—the gift for sinisterly effective Kiplingesque slogans. "We must love one another or die." Has anybody thought of a more nasty and horrid motive for our loving one another? (Just what would a love vamped up on such prudential considerations be really worth?) But it has its effectiveness as a slogan, as *telling* clap-trap, just because it leaves to the reader the choice of the level at which he wishes to interpret it. There is the level of mere platitude: "isolated people wither away." There is a level of frightful cynicism: "Though all my impulses are selfish, I need other people as a source of new energy." "I am so lonely, that I must love you, though there is nothing in you to love." There is the level of fear: "I had better love you, for otherwise you may kill me." There is even an honest level, as in Christ's answer to the rich young man who asked what should he do to inherit eternal life. "I admit that to try to love everybody, in a quite undiscriminating way, is a terrible strain and a sacrifice. But you are not forced to. You can always die . . . the more usual, and perhaps the more dignified choice." But the total effect of such slogans is *mainly* frightening, revealing a ghastly hollowness, but putting up a sort of façade in front of it, or suggesting a cheap way out. . . .

What touches the human heart is certainly not Auden's solutions (which are other people's solutions, ready-made solutions, taken over) but the situation in which Auden, and most of us, more often than we care to admit, find ourselves: that of complete isolation. Isolation is the disease, and Love, however much he cheapens the word, can still remain the word that suggests a remedy:

> Released by Love from isolating wrong
> Let us for Love unite our various song,
> Each with his gift according to his kind
> Bringing this child his body and his mind.

That is from *For the Time Being* and, according to the Christian framework of this oratorio, Love in the first line would mean charity, in the wide sense, and Love in the second God, or more precisely the Christ-child; but the effectiveness of the passage is partly due to the fact that, owing to the vague echo of the Counter-Reformation—the note of Dryden and Purcell—in the style, we *also* think of sexual love in the first line and of Cupid in the second. Thus to 'bring this child my body,' while it *ostensibly* means to bring the Christ-child a body dedicated to chastity, *also* suggests bringing Cupid a body dedicated to pleasure; this faint and trembling ambiguity creates more effective poetry than a merely Christian, or a merely pagan statement possibly could. We are aware of the death from which Auden's Love ("Winter and Love," says a more subtle poet, "are desperate medicines") is an escape; we forgive him a great deal because we, too, are aware of the "isolating wrong." Admittedly, Auden's escape has never been into personal love in the ordinary sense; rather into something larger and vaguer and more full of energy than the ordinary human situation—the dialectic (loss of oneself in history), the libido (loss of oneself in sexual ecstasy), and now God (surrender of one's will to another much more powerful one). He has been seeking situations less painful and complicated, with less of a prosaic drag about them, than this. His success as a poet, perhaps, is his failure to remain satisfied with his escapes. The pathos, what touches the human heart, is that after all these efforts the great waves move away, and the poet is as much alone as ever, lying awake in bed and regarding the other body

> Mortal, guilty, but to me
> The entirely beautiful.

Something like this perhaps is true—whether wholly intended by Auden or not—about Auden's Prospero, a Gerald Heard type, in "The Sea and the Mirror." That he quite fails (as Antonio maliciously suggests) to break his wand. There is an obvious comparison. Shakespeare was not intensely or especially a religious writer, yet in that conventional little epilogue to *The Tempest* with, as Walter de la Mare says, "its curiously apt overtones,"

> . . . now I want
> Spirits to enforce, art to enchant,
> And my ending is despair
> Unless I be relieved by prayer,
> Which pierces so, that it assaults
> Mercy itself, and frees all faults . . .

in that, we feel a consciousness of the "last things," so habitual that it does not need, so to say, to write itself up.

Auden's Prospero, on the other hand, in what might be an expansion of this passage, writes himself up to some tune.

> When the servants settle me into a chair
> In some well arranged corner of the garden
> And arrange my mufflers and rugs, shall I ever be able
> To stop myself from telling them what I am doing—
> Sailing alone, out over seventy thousand fathoms?
> Yet if I speak, I shall sink without a sound
> Into unmeaning abysses. *Can I learn to suffer*
> *Without saying something ironic or funny*
> *About suffering?*

I would say, no; the old gentleman will be talking. . . . (In passing, these three lines I have italicized show one weakness in the style of this volume—an excessive bookishness. They are like bad Aldous Huxley. They irritate because Auden's Prospero has given no evidence, sententious, loquacious, and sometimes eloquent as he is, that he is at all capable of thinking of anything very effectively ironic or funny to say; and people may be irritated, too, at the notion of suffering as a rather expensive and special luxury for the truly high-minded.)

But one sees the differences. Shakespeare is a dramatist but his people are not, in quite this sense, incessantly dramatizing themselves. For Auden the dramatic gesture (not the dramatic incident) is all important. Everything he would do would be this special sort of thing, with its sharp rhetorical edge to it—"Leave for Cape Wrath to-night!" or, "Seeing our last of Captain Ferguson." Yet ordinary common little people pray and repent, and feel the emptiness of their small successes, just as they work for a political party, or go to bed with their wives: it was not, after all, Auden who invented religion or sex or politics. Like Miranda, Auden finds novelty everywhere and everywhere assimilates it; as with her brave new world, "'tis new to *him*." This is part of what Miss Riding and Mr. Graves meant by calling him a synthetic, not a traditional, writer. Everything has to be questioned, everything explained. This partly explains the queer and rather unfeeling detachment Mr. Spender has noted: for Auden's Prospero,

> A stranger's quiet collapse in a noisy street
> Is the beginning of much lively speculation,

not the beginning of doing anything practical for the stranger.

That everything is seen from the outside, and as new, and as having to be explained (that is, as having to be set against a wider background, which is assumed, so that there may be explanations) is one reason, perhaps for certain faults of taste and feeling which are rather noticeable in *For the Time Being*. He ignores the fact that lives of ordinary routine, which look dull and simple from the outside, from the inside, broken down into their day-to-day detail, may seem interesting and complicated enough. And this causes him occasionally to indulge in a peculiarly unpleasant mixture of spiritual and social snobbery:

> The solitude familiar to the poor
> Is feeling that the family next door
> The way it talks, eats, dresses, loves, and hates
> Is indistinguishable from one's own.

Both the facts, and the values implied here, seem to me wrong. It is the upper classes in all ages, who have tended to conventionalize their behaviour; Goldsmith somewhere has an acute remark about the manners of the gentry being the same all over eighteenth-century Europe—one must look both for national characteristics, and individual eccentricities, among the peasantry. I am sure, I am much more *like* any other middle-class intellectual of my age, than a plumber in Bradford is like a plumber in London. Secondly, I do not see what is wrong with the family next door being like my family. Real conversation, real intimacy, is, in fact, only possible when two people share a general background of behaviour, and indeed of reading, and of taste, which is so much taken for granted that it need not be talked about. The individualism which Auden *seems* to be advocating here is rather like that which, along so many English streets, jostles together the fake-Tudor or neo-lavatorial pub, the commercial Renaissance bank, and the jazz-modernistic cinema. I prefer the amenity of the Georgian crescent. An even more snobbish (and very badly written) passage is this

> Redeem for the dull the
> Average Way
> That common ungifted
> Natures may
> Believe that their normal
> Vision can
> Walk to perfection.

It is not really such a colossal and crushing tragedy not to be Mr. Auden; and the best of us are very common and ungifted, in very many directions, and the most limited of us is capable of sacrifice and love.

This stuffiness is all the more depressing when one remembers Auden's former gift, in a poem like "August for the people and their favourite islands," of summing up, quite easily and lazily, the whole atmosphere of a place and the people there; and he seems to have lost that, and to have lost the unaffected pleasure he once felt in the sight of people being easily and lazily themselves; America could have offered him Coney Island, instead of these depressing and unconvincing generalizations, but the American scene, the American atmosphere, the speech habits of America, appear not to exist for him. I think there is a reason, a sociological one. The façade of English life is a very composed one, the flaws in the surface are difficult to detect, and one of the things that made Auden before the war a poet of such extreme social significance was his ability to put a finger on points of extreme, but hidden, stress. But America does not present a composed façade; it makes a cult, almost, of the incongruous; it is almost blind to the incongruous; and American writers tend, like Henry Adams, or the Southern Regionalists, either to invent a manner adapted to a composed society which doesn't exist, but ought to, or like Sinclair Lewis, in his earlier and less regrettable days, to shout at the top of their voices to draw attention to incongruities which, even for the least sensitive English observer, would be glaring enough. A writer like Auden for instance, or like Rex Warner, might do a fruitful parody of a leader in *The Times,* the *Economist,* or the *Spectator;* but a leader in the *Saturday Evening Post* parodies itself. There is a degree of rusticity which exhausts the resources of language. In America, I suppose, there are only three alternatives: one surrenders, one becomes hysterical and hoarse like Mark Twain or Sinclair Lewis, or one withdraws. Auden seems to have withdrawn, and America, for all it exists for him, might be a desert island. There is only one outbreak of the old beautiful malice and mischief, a poem which I first read in a scribbled copy over a bar in Cairo:

> In the Retreat from Reason he deserted on his rocking horse
> And lived on a fairy's kindness till he tired of kicking her,
> He smashed her spectacles and stole her cheque-book and mackintosh
> Then cruised his way back to the Army.
> *George, you old numero,*
> *How did you get in the Army?*

That is nicely done. But, on the whole, and at least for the time being, Auden seems to have lost that promise he had once of being our best poet in a conversational style (that is, our best poet with an adult social sense) since the Byron of "Don Juan" or perhaps even since Pope.

On the other hand, Auden is steadily increasing his mastery over the actual craft of verse. There is almost no form, no metre at which he is not capable of having a pretty competent try. His most interesting metrical innovation in "The Sea and the Mirror" is the borrowing of syllabic metre from Miss Marianne Moore. He uses this in what is perhaps his most perfect single poem to date, "Alonso to Ferdinand." Each line has exactly nine syllables, the stanzas have an elaborate and difficult rhyme scheme, but since stressed can rhyme with unstressed syllables the number of possible full rhymes in English is greatly extended; the general effect of the metre, in Auden's use of it, is to give an effect of careful but successful concentration, like a military slow march with the soldiers counting their steps, or like counting your steps when you are dancing a slow waltz. His use of the metre is quite unlike Miss Moore's who always has the air of balancing, say, a pile of plates which are always about to topple over but never quite do; the air of doing something surprising, difficult, acrobatic, sometimes almost (elegantly) clownish . . . indulging, as she does, in lines of varying length and slyly concealed rhyme patterns. Auden's use of the metre is more straightforward, his effect smooth, grave, and majestic. I think syllabic metre is a very important and useful innovation in English verse . . . much more so, for instance, than Hopkins' type of metre, which tends to distort the natural syntax and cadence of the English language, and can only be used effectively, indeed, in Hopkins's own peculiar type of rhetoric. It would be a mistake, of course, to attempt to read "Alonso to Ferdinand" without any stresses at all; what the reader will find himself stressing is what the French call the "mobile accent" . . . or those words on which, from the sense pattern (of the individual line, not of the sentence or paragraph) there is a natural rhetorical stress. That stress, however, will be a modulated one, so as not to rack the slow and grave syllabic pattern.

With this advance in metrical accomplishment there goes, however, that tendency towards an impressive vagueness, even towards a triteness or woolliness, of metaphor and simile first noticed by Julian Symons. The contrast with the tightness of Auden's earliest poems is striking and from some points of view depressing. "My dear one is mine as mirrors are lonely." That, as reviewer after reviewer has pointed out, is a very lovely line. But just how does my dear one being mine resemble mirrors being lonely? (To anybody with some knowledge of how poems are composed, it must seem possible that Auden may have written first, "My dear one is mine *though* mirrors are lonely," and then, by the alteration of a syllable, created at once a more euphonious and a more mysterious line.) It might be a mere comparison of degree: mirrors are so lonely that they reflect everything which is in front of them, and my dear one just as completely reflects me (or I may be, indeed, comparing myself to the mirror; I am so lonely for my dear one as a mirror is for everything, and for me there is nothing else, my dear one is everything). That is enough to satisfy the syntax, but the sadness and the beauty of the line come partly, I think, from the fact that mirrors are so obvious a symbol both of understanding and separation; I am reflected completely in the mirror, but I also, my real self, remain completely outside the mirror; or, in love with you, I reflect you completely, but you are free, as a person, to move away, while I still possess—for a little time—your image. And if *both* you and I are like mirrors, we only know each other as reflected in each other, and being in love is important as a way of possessing oneself. But this possession is illusory, for the surface never melts away, never quite dissolves even in love, and we can never, like Alice, enter the looking-glass kingdom, and wander together there, hand in hand. All these ideas are more or less relevant, and there are probably others I have missed. The point is that one can't, of course, stop to work them all out while actually reading the poem. One has the impression, merely, of something moving, intricate, and perhaps true, and passes on. This intricate vagueness has its own fascination and I cannot agree with Mr. Symons in regarding it as mere laziness on Auden's part. He knows very well, I should think, its peculiar effectiveness.

I have been delaying coming to grips with Auden's thought. William Empson has a striking little poem, "Reflection from Rochester," in which he says that the mind

> . . . now less easily decides
> On a good root confusion to amass
> Much safety from irrelevent despair.
> Mere change in numbers made the process crass.

Auden is not a thinker in the sense that Empson is; but what he has really been doing all along is seeking, in politics, or psychology, or religion, for a good root-confusion which would make the despair (which is, I think, his centrally important experience) irrelevant. Partly for that reason his politics, his psychology, and now his religion are always off-centre. And they are, in fact, confusing. They are ways both of explaining and of attempting to get rid of—but also to infect others with a personal sense of guilt. He does seek in that sense, in Sykes Davies' phrase, to solidify personal neuroses. The particular type of religious thinking to be found in *For the Time Being* is not new in his work. It is to be found in the famous poem that begins,

> Sir, no man's enemy, forgiving all
> But will his negative inversion, be prodigal . . .

and that ends with the rather undergraduate line,

> New styles of architecture, a change of heart.

It is a religion of emotional conversion, and, among historical forms of Christianity, it resembles Lutheranism more than either Roman Catholicism or High Calvinism. It makes much more of God's will and less of His reason, much more of the individual's direct response to God and less of the idea of fellowship in a Church, than Roman Catholicism, but it does allow some scope for man's emotions (if not for his reasonable will) to co-operate with God, and it does not go all the way with that type of extreme Protestantism which makes man's salvation or damnation *entirely* dependent upon God's particular election. The general effect of such a religion would be to make men feel that, whether or not necessarily wicked, they are certainly weak, and that perhaps it is better to sin strongly and to repent strongly than to be puffed up with a sense of one's strength and virtue. (Herod, the good administrator, in Auden's oratorio, is the man who tries to rely on his own will and reasoned moral standards; he is rather venomously treated. Caesar, in another poem, stands for all man's attempts to stand on his own feet—in science, in culture, in philosophy, as well as in politics—and it is made clear that from Auden's standpoint all these are equally wicked and disastrous.) The dangers of this particular type of religion, with its emphasis on some sort of emotional surrender, are seen more clearly in "The Sea and the Mirror." Antonio's great crime is that he has not surrendered to Prospero,

> Your all is partial, Prospero;
> My will is all my own;
> Your need to love shall never know
> Me; I am I, Antonio:
> My choice myself alone.

But if Prospero can be a symbol for God, he might also be a symbol for Hitler. No man has the right to compel another man's love, unless he can prove himself worthy of it; no God either, for that matter, unless he can prove that, as well as being powerful, he is good. "God is not without sin. He created the World," says an old proverb from the East, and it is not very noble to worship a God just because he is powerful and can harm us. Auden, indeed, does show that he is aware of this dilemma:

> Alone, alone, about a dreadful wood
> Of conscious evil runs a lost mankind,
> Dreading to find its Father lest it find
> The Goodness it has dreaded is not good . . .

but his solution is Kierkegaard's, that of the emotional leap in the dark, not Milton's, that of justifying the ways of God to man. We have seen some of the results of the emotional leap in the dark in politics (and German politics have suffered greatly from the tradition of passive obedience that goes with Lutheran pietism) and German politics, when Hitler played Prospero, suffered greatly from the lack of a few Antonios. Auden has perhaps found a temporary solution for a number of his own personal difficulties, but I do not think that he has lighted on a very useful root-confusion for the rest of us. He seems to me, on the whole, to be *less* illuminating than in the days of his psychological and political probings.

He is not, I think, fundamentally a religious poet, any more than, for example, Milton was.[1] A person with the genuine piety, the sense of mystery and awe, of, say, Dr. Johnson could never have made out of the truths of the Christian religion the purely mythological pattern—the argumentative deity and the cannonading angels of *Paradise Lost*. The artist and the dialectician were strong enough in Milton to make use of this dangerous material and the artist and the dialectician are strong enough in Auden. But I find no evidence anywhere in this book of Auden's, any more than anywhere in Milton, of any profound *personal* spiritual experience; such as one finds, for instance, in Mr. David Gascoyne's *Noctambules* or in some short poems of Miss Kathleen Raine's. He is not a religious poet in that sense, and though *For the Time Being* has some affinities with *The Rock,* I do not see Auden going on to write something like *Four Quartets*. His gifts are of another sort, and his strength is of another sort. Antonio's mockery is true,

> Antonio, sweet brother, has to laugh.
> How easy you have made it to refuse
> Peace to your greatness! Break your wand in half,
> The fragments will join; burn your books or lose

[1] I hope this doesn't sound too paradoxical. The distinction is between grasping a theology as a coherent parable, or a coherent system of ideas, which is what Milton and Auden do, and having a certain kind of personal experience, a sharp and immediate sense of goodness or of evil. Or perhaps it might be described as the difference between generalized and personal experience, between accepting a set of ideas because on the whole they seem to fit, and being absolutely gripped and held by a certain sort of experience. Neither Auden nor Milton seem to be gripped and held. They choose, rather, to grip and hold. They could let go.

Because they could let go, poets like Auden and Milton are more anxious to persuade than poets, like Herbert, or Vaughan, or Crashaw, of actual religious experience. One does not need to argue about actual experience. One has had it, and can merely attempt to record it.

Them in the sea, they will soon reappear
Not even damaged: as long as I choose
To wear my fashion, whatever you wear
Is a magic robe. . . .

We can allow no peace to Auden's greatness. He will not be satisfied until he has written something which is utterly moving, persuading, convincing to *everybody,* and, of course, he will never do this. There will always be the schoolboy who doesn't attend, the scout who skips the parade, the man who chooses dying instead of loving, the heckler with the awkward question, the fellow conjuror chiefly interested in how he does the trick—there will always be Antonio. Prospero, again and again, will have to postpone the breaking of his wand. But, after all, is it to be regretted? There are so many professional mystagogues; so many dull preachers; so many cheapjacks with their bottled spiritual cure-alls; but of all poets writing today, there is only Auden with just that range and scope. His strength is not in what he accepts, but in what he discards. It lies just as much in a certain fundamental ruthlessness as in the love about which he talks so vaguely and so much. He is a much greater man than his ideas; as a poet, a major voice, as a thinker, about on the level of Mr. Middleton Murry. Because he has a major voice, what he says will always be relevant, without having to be, in a sense, true. (In one sense, it always will be true; it will always be a possible synthesis of an unusually wide reading and experience—it will always be pragmatically true, a possible "working scheme." "All I have is a voice. . . ."

III. *Auden's Later Manner*

Of all the poets whom I have dealt with in this volume, I feel that I have treated Mr. Auden least fairly. Irritation not so much with his ideas as with his manner of entertaining ideas has, through the years, when I have had occasion to deal with him, betrayed me into a carping, petulant, suspicious tone; and I am now beginning to see that to argue whether his ideas were right or wrong had as little to do with the strict function of a critic of poetry as treating, for instance, Dryden's *Religio Laici* or Tennyson's *In Memoriam* as pamphlets about natural religion, to be supported or refuted by logical arguments. I tended, in all my earlier writing about Mr. Auden, to take elements in a composition for statements in a pulpit, or a witness-box. I nagged at a social attitude which irritated me, where I should have taken the social attitude as "given," and reverted to it only when I thought some inadequacy in it helped to explain some inadequacy in what was poetically made of it. Let me try, now, to make some belated slight amends.

He does remain, of course, the most considerable Anglo-American poet of his generation. As Mr. Richard Hoggart says, in an admirable recent British Council Pamphlet about him, one still hesitates to accord him major status—to put him "up there," as it were, with Yeats, with his own early master, Hardy, with Mr. Eliot—but he does remain, at fifty or so, the most exciting and promising "younger poet" of our generation. Nobody else of around the same age—except in his narrower but perhaps sometimes deeper mode, Mr. Empson—rivals him in speculative agility or technical adroitness. And Mr. Empson has written only three or four new poems since 1940. Nobody at all, of all poets who are active now, rivals Mr. Auden in fertility of invention. And yet, I suppose, over the last ten years or so few of us have been wholly happy about the way his poetry has been going. I shall say nothing about *The Age of Anxiety*. A learned Italian critic, Signor Melchiori, in his book *The Tightrope Walkers,* thinks of it as a triumph in a new baroque manner, square and solid in construction, but with lavish extravagant ornamentation; it uses a very primitive metrics, that of Anglo-Saxon poetry, for a very sophisticated theme: and I remember a fine scholar saying to me, when it first came out, "If one is seeking to be 'mannerist,' to play on one's sense of the jarring inappropriateness of subject to handling, of content to form, why not instead try out the metre of *Hiawatha*?" But two volumes of shorter poems, largely of "light" poems, *Nones* and *The Shield of Achilles,* deserve both a warmer welcome and a more respectful consideration.

Let me take the second of these volumes first, *The Shield of Achilles.* And let me relate it to the two aspects of Mr. Auden's work which have most worried recent critics. One of these is a growing lack of personal immediacy; the other is an over-piling of verbal ornament. That lack of immediacy is very noticeable, for instance, in the first seven poems in *The Shield of Achilles,* the set called "Bucolics." These are like the notes of a very intelligent lecturer in human ecology done into verse. Thus, when we turn to the poem (among the poems on plains, mountains, and so forth) on islands, we do not get a vivid image like Mr. Pound's

> Tawn foreshores
> Washed in the cobalt of oblivions.

We get instead reflections, pungent, intelligent, but faintly chilling, on penal colonies and dying Pacific races:

> Once, where detected worldlings now
> Do penitential jobs,
> Exterminated species played
> Who had not read their Hobbes.

Nothing could be neater but (as in the fine "Ode to Gaea" in another section) it is our world seen from an aeroplane. The poet, on the whole, brackets his personal life off from his poetry. We find ourselves longing for some concentration of direct experience, out of which the generalizations could grow.

Mr. Auden, of course, has always been a generalizer. He has never been interested either in his own experience, or the experience of other people, for its own sake; he has been interested in it as an instance of a general case, of the sort of thing that happens. He has a classifying mind; he is at the very, very extreme opposite pole from a poet like Hopkins with his passionate concentration on *haecceitas,* thisness, "sakes," "selving" and "unselving," "inscape." The worry that critics may have had about his attitude to language in his recent books is not about this "given" element in him; it is about a painstaking frivolity, a preoccupation with ornament. He does manfully defend the baroque mode:

> Be subtle, various, ornamental, clever,
> And do not listen to those critics ever
> Whose crude provincial gullets crave in books
> Plain cooking made still plainer by plain cooks. . . .

Walter Bagehot was one of "those critics" and I agree with Bagehot that the way to make a basket of fish poetical is *not* by calling it, as Tennyson did in *Enoch Arden,*

> . . . Enoch's ocean-spoil
> In ocean-smelling osier. . . .

Or that way of handling it *does,* of course, make it "poetical": but in a soppily vulnerable way, a way for the tough and wry who hate poetry to kick at.

Let us consider, with this suspicion of "the poetical" in mind, such a passage as this of Mr. Auden's, from his recent work:

> The horn gate and the ivory gate
> Swing to, swing shut, instantaneously
> Quell the nocturnal rummage
> Of its rebellious fronde, ill-favoured,
> Ill-natured and second-rate,
> Disenfranchised, widowed and orphaned
> By an historical mistake. . . .

But for the Fall, the basic sense of that passage is, our dreams would not be Freudian dreams—would not be so shabby, guilty, and incoherent as they are (the shabbiness expressed by "nocturnal rummage," "rebellious fronde," and so on: the Fall, ironically, by "an historical mistake"). The rhetoric, the mechanisms of persuasion, in such a passage is one of expansion; the plain, underlying prose sense is "like gold to ayery thinness beat"; the lines *look* as if they were making a much more portentous and complex statement than they are making.

The title poem of *The Shield of Achilles,* a grim meditation on power politics, perhaps on the *Iliad* itself as what Simone Weil called "the Poem of Force," had a bleak impressiveness: three victims being (not exactly) crucified:

> The mass and majesty of this world, all
> That carries weight and always weighs the same
> Lay in the hands of others; they were small
> And could not hope for help and no help came:
> What their foes liked to do was done, their shame
> Was all the worst could wish; they lost their pride
> And died as men before their bodies died.

That impresses me poetically, impresses me morally, and yet there is something about the attitude implied in it that very frighteningly raises the whole question, in the context of which in the 1930s one always, perhaps obtusely, would discuss Mr. Auden's poetry of the power of poetic perception to influence events. An hour or so before I copied out these lines I read, in *The Manchester Guardian,* a translation of passages from M. Alleg's book, *La Question.* M. Alleg is the editor of a Communist newspaper, who was tortured by parachutists in Algeria. His torturers told him that they were modelling themselves on the Gestapo, that they hoped to torture Frenchmen, including liberal or radical political leaders, in France, too, and be done with the Republic. I reflected that if there is any country in Europe which men of other countries have turned to as a centre of civilization, have loved second to their own countries, it is France. I reflected also that as at least a sympathizer with Communism M. Alleg must have in his time turned a Nelson eye to the possibility that men were being tortured behind the Iron Curtain; and yet, standing up to torture himself, he seemed to speak not as a partisan but for all men. In a sense, Auden speaks also in these lines for all men—but hopelessly? In the 1930s, he seemed often ahead of events, warning us of what we might still do to dodge our fates. In a poem like *The Shield of Achilles,* he is like the chorus in a Greek tragedy, which makes all the appropriate moral comments, but knows it cannot prevent the awful thing happening. By classical standards, this should make him a more universal poet; and by revealing starkly what is worst in us, he may in fact, in such a poem, be nerving us to pursue what is better. And yet, in a cruder way, did he not move us more when he took sides more, when he seemed to speak with even crude power, like an orator? Was "the preacher's loose, immodest tone," which he once often protested against, not part of his early power over one?

In fact, the vein which I often find most attractive in Mr. Auden's later poems is not this harsh, bleak vein but one of playfulness. There was much of this in the volume which preceded *The Shield of Achilles,* the volume called *Nones,* the most variously pleasurable for me of all Mr. Auden's more recent volumes. Nones is the daily office of the Church originally said at the ninth hour, or three o'clock in the afternoon; it was between the sixth and the ninth hour, while Christ hung on the Cross, that there was a darkness over the earth, the sun was darkened, and the veil of the Temple was rent. So far, certainly, the title does not suggest a mood of cheerfulness. But there is another meaning of the word more directly relevant to the mood of at least the lighter pieces in the book. "Nones" is the old spelling of "nonce." Many of the poems in *Nones* are nonce-poems (poems inspired by unrecurring occasions or written, in some cases, for public declaration at American graduation ceremonies): many of these are also full of nonce-words:

> On the mountain, the baltering torrent
> Sunk to a soodling thread,

for instance; the once battering but now faltering torrent sunk, I suppose, to a soothing and dawdling thread. One is half tempted on reading such lines to wonder whether Mr. Auden's inspiration has itself begun to soodle, but, if there was little or nothing in *Nones* in Mr. Auden's old, urgent, hortatory vein, that was because of a feeling that all "sane affirmative speech" has been so "pawed-at" and "profaned" by newspapers and politicians that the only civilized tone of voice for a poet today is

> . . . the wry, the sotto voce,
> Ironic and monochrome.

And in fact Mr. Auden has rarely written with more confident ease than in the lighter pieces in *Nones*. He hits just the note he wants to, even when he is seeking to hold the restless attention of an audience of undergraduates:

> Between the chances, choose the odd;
> Read *The New Yorker,* trust in God;
> And take short views.

Whether under the ease of the surface of such poems there is a slackness of will is another question; also, how far irony and humour at this level can unconsciously betray an undue complacency of spirit. There is a *New Yorker* side to Mr. Auden, and the recipe for the *New Yorker* type of humour is to step far enough back from the routines we are all immersed in to feel sophisticated about them; but not far enough back to cease to be one of the boys. But Auden can be one of the boys at several levels and there is a quite different snob highbrow pleasure, for instance, in recognizing the tessellations of Horatian syntax in these lines addressed to Mr. Brian Howard:

> . . . what bees
> From the blossoming chestnut
> Or short but shapely dark-haired men
>
> From the aragonian grape distil, your amber wine,
> Your coffee-coloured honey. . . .

To read a volume like *Nones* is, in fact, to recognize once again that Mr. Auden is more adroit—almost unscrupulously adroit, perhaps—than anyone else now writing verse; he can be back-slapping, ominous, port-winy, or abstruse, as the occasion demands. Yet even where he does not aim at major statements, there are major themes, above all the Christian theme, in the background; the frivolity is in a sense permissible because the last things, death, judgment, hell, heaven, are always in Mr.

Auden's mind, and the worldly hopes men set their hearts upon have been rejected. In the interim, there is nothing against a little harmless enjoyment. Mr. Auden's type of Christianity strikes me, as I have said in an earlier essay, as being a sophisticated Lutheranism. He does not exactly say to us, *Pecca fortiter,* but to avoid despair he has put most of his money on Grace since he knows he is going to fall down on Works. One trouble about such a type of Christianity is that to the outsider it might not seem to make much practical difference:

> But that Miss Number in the corner
> Playing hard to get . . .
> I am sorry I'm not sorry . . .
> Make me chaste, Lord, but not yet.

Humility consists of recognizing one's impurity, but also provides an excuse for going on being impure:

> The Love that rules the sun and stars
> Permits what he forbids.

I saw the poem from which these lines come first in typescript. Auden had sent it to a Roman Catholic lady, a friend of mine, who was editing a literary magazine and she was embarrassed, much admiring Auden's work generally, but feeling that the allusions to St. Augustine and Dante in that jazzy context were in desperately bad taste; I agreed with her then, but now feel that I was silly and squeamish. It is one of the strengths of Auden's handling of the theme of Grace and Original Sin that he doesn't worry about shocking *les bien pensants.* And when he expresses, as he sometimes does, his more intimate and personal convictions, he can be very moving, as in these lines from one of the most beautiful of all his recent poems, the loveliest poem in *Nones,* "In Praise of Limestone":

> Dear, I know nothing of
> Either, but when I try to imagine a faultless love
> Or the life to come, what I hear is the murmur
> Of underground streams, what I see is a limestone landscape.

Nones was a disconcerting book, but I would say it more often embodied positive values (it is certainly a value that somebody can go on unashamedly enjoying himself today, as Mr. Auden seems to) than *The*

Age of Anxiety, where the theme of our awkward *malaise* was all too faithfully mirrored—Professor Ivor Winter's "fallacy of imitative form" —in the elaborately maladroit handling. From all sorts of official and respectable points of view, *Nones* was a quietly outrageous little book, and one liked it all the more for that. Deliberately slackening down a little when everybody else is keyed up, taking a humorous view of guilt and anxiety as part of the set-up—"throwing it away," as the actors say of a strong line—is, after all, a defensible human attitude when everybody else is getting shrill, frightened, and nasty. But one's admiration for Auden, from first to last, remains mingled with doubts. From his beginnings, he could be spotted as a potentially major talent: will the moment come, or has it come already, or is it too late for it to come now, when we shall look back on all that he has done and salute a major achievement? Or will he always remain for critics the problem prodigy, the boy who "might have gone anywhere," but who always, when the obvious goals were pointed out to him, chose to go somewhere else?

Introduction to Auden's Poetry

by Richard Hoggart

I. *Early Life and Background; Characteristic Moods and Settings; the Landscapes of Home and of Wandering*

W. H. Auden was born at York, in 1907, into a professional middle-class family. His father was a Medical Officer of Health with wide interests. The family soon moved to Birmingham, where Auden gained first-hand experience of economic depression. He was given an education typical of his class and time. He went to a public school (Gresham's, Holt, Norfolk) and so to Oxford University in the middle Twenties. At school he talked first of being an engineer and read books on mining and geology (the contrast with the vocation of poet is not, in Auden's case, as striking as it might seem at first sight). In his later years at school Auden began to write poetry. Thomas Hardy was his first model, a good model since Hardy is a splendid and idiosyncratic versifier and a deeply humane writer. Hardy is also an uneven poet; as Auden has remarked, he does not discourage a young poet by showing consistent technical mastery. At his Oxford college, Christ Church, Auden wrote poetry continually and by then was claiming that T. S. Eliot was the only fit modern exemplar for a young poet. He began to acquire a reputation as a "character." He helped to edit *Oxford Poetry,* an annual collection. After leaving Oxford he spent some time in pre-Hitler Germany (the Germany of Christopher Isherwood's *Goodbye to Berlin*); the grim Thirties were just beginning. Once back in England, Auden was for a short time a schoolmaster and seems to have deeply enjoyed it. He has much of the teacher in his com-

"Introduction to Auden's Poetry." From *W. H. Auden: A Selection* (London: Hutchinson Educational, Ltd., 1961) by Richard Hoggart, pp. 17-41 of the Introduction. This introduces a selection of Auden's poetry "chiefly intended for study by senior pupils in schools" (p. 13). Grateful acknowledgment is made to Random House, Inc. and Faber & Faber, Ltd. for permission to reprint the four complete poems by W. H. Auden included in Mr. Hoggart's essay.

position: he likes explaining things; he can be sympathetic without being sentimental, interested and affectionate towards people without being soft; he has a disciplinary streak.

He is deeply attached also to the English landscape. This might seem so common an attachment as not to be worth noticing. Yet sometimes we say we like the English scene without being clear just what we like, or perhaps have a stereotyped picture of thatched cottages and winding lanes. Auden knew quite early what kinds of landscape he likes and why. He likes, first, industrial landscapes, densely packed landscapes which are pockmarked with the evidence of intensive human endeavour and ingenuity—"the soiled productive cities" of the Black Country, the mining areas, the Lancashire cotton-belt (he once said that the view of Lancashire's mills from the top of the Pennines was one of the finest man-made sights in the world). "Tramlines and slagheaps, pieces of machinery/That was, and is, my ideal scenery," he wrote. All such landscapes bring home to him that man is a maker, a struggling but inventive creature using mind and hands and making a home wherever there is suitable space to settle. This interest dominates almost all Auden's geographical passages. He is only rarely interested in natural scenes for or in themselves; his geography is almost always human—economic or political—geography (as in *Macao* or *Spain*). What, he asks, does this landscape mean to men? What history have they stamped on it? In such passages his landscape is a backcloth to human activity.

Auden likes also bare and upland settings, especially mountainous regions wrested into stark and improbable shapes by glacial action. He loved walking with his father in the upper Pennines and during much of his time in New York, years later, his bedside book was a study of the mineralogy of the Lake District. He rarely refers to what might be called typical Sussex countryside or to that kind of landscape which—though it is not the only kind he describes—we often find in Tennyson, a rich and heavy landscape of hollyhocks and warm meadows (see *Dover, 1937*). If Auden's landscape is to be cluttered he prefers it to be cluttered with the evidence of man's industrial toil; if it is to be bare he prefers it bleakly bare. To this bare landscape he is drawn not only for itself but because, as he might well say, it speaks to him; it becomes symbolic for him in a way we must consider later. By instinct he thinks through images of landscape; he speaks of "villages of the heart," "suburbs of fear" and "our landscape of pain"—sometimes so easily that it seems almost automatic.

If we had space to suggest only one picture of Auden, and if this picture had to be as nearly as possible representative, we would show a landscape and a wanderer, a man on a Quest (as in the *Quest* sonnets). The figure of the Wanderer, the isolated man on a search, appears more frequently than any other in Auden's poetry. The Wanderer can take many forms. In the earliest verse he may be called the Airman or the Leader or the Hawk. He is physically isolated and surveys from a great height the interesting but muddled life of those below; he can see a possible order in the muddle which they do not see, and he would like to help it emerge. He is detached and slightly clinical. He is compassionate but also rather coldly reformative. Auden's is a strongly abstracting and generalizing intelligence; thought he loves particular details, he wants always to relate them to a larger pattern. He does not naturally possess a loving submission to particular things in themselves, to the varied "thisness" of life (the word is from G. M. Hopkins, who loved the "thisness" of individual things); and he often too quickly *uses* his observation of individual human habits, rather than sits before them in humility.

Or the Wanderer may move across vast and empty landscapes—plains, mountains, the spaces of the sea. It is entirely typical that Auden's one volume of prose criticism, *The Enchafèd Flood* (1951), should be about sea and desert imagery and symbolic wanderings across them; and one of the first operas for which he wrote the libretto was *The Rake's Progress*—in Auden's version the Rake becomes, again, a Wanderer across the face of the earth. But usually Auden's Wanderer is not so much escaping challenges as positively seeking order.

So one might follow the Wanderer figure throughout Auden's poetry, or one might follow the varying appearances of his landscapes. One would constantly see the two as interlinked. A group of recent poems is called simply *Bucolics,* poems about landscapes. Here the landscapes are of that second, symbolic kind mentioned briefly above. Auden, we have seen, has a mind which naturally makes patterns and symbols. He discovered early that involved or geometrically patterned landscapes, or the relations between types of landscape (plains and mountains; valley and sea), pulled at him with a strength which could not be adequately explained by such a phrase as "the attraction of natural beauty." They seemed to make visible to his imagination—without at first being consciously formulated—the shapes of struggles within the human will. They were symbols of human dilemmas, though he had not deliberately tried to make them into symbols.

In some of these later landscape poems Auden has used a long loping line which follows the movement of his thought as he explores the peculiar symbolic hold the landscape has upon him. We may see this by looking more closely at part of the poem *In Praise of Limestone*:

> If it form the one landscape that we the inconstant ones
> Are consistently homesick for, this is chiefly
> Because it dissolves in water. Mark these rounded slopes
> With their surface fragrance of thyme and beneath
> A secret system of caves and conduits; hear these springs
> That spurt out everywhere. . . .
> . . . examine this region
> Of short distances and definite places—

The long verse-sentence has an easy spoken quality; it mixes colloquialism and serious observation, wit and moral concern—though sometimes the tone relaxes into a deliberate facetiousness. The poem's shape and its sinuous movement act out, as it were, the meditation within the poet's mind. As he looks at these large limestone hills above the wide plains and the fertile valleys, the scene becomes both actually and symbolically moving to him; it begins to stand for some of the complex struggles, the tensions, in human wills and motives—between man's urge to settle and domesticate, and his urge to wander; between men as quiet and gregarious beings and men as isolated or power-seeking beings; between those who think they can tame life and those who listen to deeper rhythms:

> Adjusted to the local needs of valleys
> Where everything can be touched or reached by walking,
> Their eyes have never looked into infinite space. . . .
> That is why, I suppose,
> The best and worst never stayed here long but sought
> Immoderate soils where the beauty was not so external,
> The light less public and the meaning of life
> Something more than a mad camp. "Come!" cried the granite wastes. . . .

So the poem explores this landscape and these relationships and closes on a view in perspective of the statues ("useless" to our puritan or utilitarian minds, but not without meaning) that man makes out of this same soft rock:

> But if
> Sins can be forgiven, if bodies rise from the dead,
> These modifications of matter into

Innocent athletes and gesticulating fountains,
  Made solely for pleasure, make a further point:
The blessed will not care what angle they are regarded from,
  Having nothing to hide. Dear, I know nothing of
Either, but when I try to imagine a faultless love
  Or the life to come, what I hear is the murmur
Of underground streams, what I see is a limestone landscape.

This is only one of the latest in a long line of Auden's landscapes, as we have seen—landscapes with many variations but also with certain clearly defined dominant characteristics. Across them the Wanderer moves, remembering his home fondly but driven on by a desire to find order and meaning. There is much in the figure that is plainly Auden himself, on a search which now seems to occupy him more than the pursuit of poetic excellence—the search for a life nearer to God's purposes. But that search had begun a long time ago. It can be seen, if we now use hindsight, in the very first poem in our selection ("From the very first coming down"). And though the particular preoccupations of the Thirties may have obscured it, it was there also throughout that time.

II. *Auden in the Thirties; Social and Psychological Observation; "Objective Reporting" and Conversational Verse*

Auden's first volume, *Poems,* appeared in 1930, at the opening of a decade which is now beginning to acquire a slightly "period" flavour, especially for those not old enough to have known it. What sort of a decade was it, to those who knew it as young adults? It was, first, a peculiarly well-defined or boldly marked period. "A time of crisis and dismay" Auden called it, and no other poet so captured the "climate" of that time.

At home, unemployment grew sharply as the effects of the Wall Street Crash of 1929 spread into Europe. Unemployment hung massively over the decade until the effort of rearmament in its later years brought some dubious alleviation. This was the period of Depressed Areas and Means Tests, of "The Threadbare Common Man / Begot on Hire-Purchase by Insurance." It was, for far too many people—for the unemployed who marched from Jarrow in the North to state their case in London, for those who hung idle round street-corner lamp-posts, for the wives making do on little money about whom George Orwell wrote in *The Road to Wigan Pier,* for the shabby clerks and graduates who peddled gimcrack Japanese household goods from door to door—it was for all these a squalid and disheartened period.

Internationally, it was an even more menacing period, since it saw a giant's march to the world war of 1939-45. In Europe Mussolini had been the first of the major dictators to assume power; he was followed and soon surpassed by Hitler who became German Chancellor in 1933. The decade's crucial middlepoint was the start of the Spanish Civil War in 1936, a dress rehearsal for 1939 (see *Spain, 1937*). Many who watched this sequence of events were horrified and alarmed at the rapid drift towards war. Yet many others, and of these some in the British Government, were inclined to minimize it and to talk of the effectiveness of "appeasement." These were the political members of what Auden called "the old gang."

In such a situation politics, domestic and international, were bound to loom large for intelligent and articulate young people. Auden belonged to a traditionally concerned group: that of the academically trained, professional class intellectuals. He and those other poets who soon became known as The Auden Group (it was a community of ideas, not of mutually planned actions) were prepared to spend time on "the flat ephemeral pamphlet and the boring meeting." So this is also the period of the Popular Front meetings, of the Left Book Club and of Aid for Spain. There was, it is true, something rather too easily dramatic about much of this interest; it lent itself to a comfortably exciting "goodies and baddies" feeling, a feeling that "the old gang" were always hopelessly out of touch and wrong, and the new boys on the political Left always on the side of the angels. Yet the basic impulse was generous and charitable.

More important in any study of Auden, one has to be careful not to overestimate the extent, or misunderstand the nature, of his political commitment. He *was* politically interested and active; he did go to Spain for a short time during the Civil War; he did visit China to see the Sino-Japanese War at first-hand (see *Journey to a War*). Yet his political interest was always subordinate to his interest in the nature of man himself, in the roots of his social and individual problems; that is, in metaphysics. In the Thirties this interest often showed itself also as an attention to psychology (as in such poems as *Petition* and *A Free One*). He talked much of Freud and of many other psychologists; he interested himself particularly in loneliness, anxiety and fear, in "the lost, the lonely, the unhappy." We can now see that at bottom this concern was religious.

But there was, Auden and other writers felt, a specific and urgent job to be done in the Thirties. They had to look at their society and write about it as incisively as they could. Geoffrey Grigson, one of the most influential editors of the decade, exhorted them to be "objective"; "Report well. Begin with objects and events," he urged. With this view Auden had much sympathy. He too exhorted his friends to be more "clinical," to seek "objective speech," to beware of romanticism and the excessively personal. We may well feel that such an attitude came more easily to Auden than to some of his friends (Stephen Spender, for instance). So much of Auden's verse at any time is in a sense detached, impersonal, briskly purposive. Some of his Thirties verse is spiritually muscular, a sort of moral gymnastics.

But the pressures of the day also helped to strengthen certain more valuable capacities in Auden. He has a naturally sharp eye for detail, for the revealing detail which indicates a habit of mind, a way of life, the nature of a social group:

> And nervous people who will never marry
> Live upon dividends in the old-world cottages
> With an animal for friend or a volume of memoirs.

It is acute, pithy, well observed. It is also a little too smart, too much like pinning and labelling a beetle. At its best, Auden's social and psychological observation of the Thirties produces—to use a phrase he would probably be happy to have applied to his poetry—"memorable speech." When the poems work well they capture outlooks and settings in a way we do not easily forget. Auden cannot, however, usually sustain this kind of insight and control at length; we tend to remember isolated lines, couplets and stanzas (or a few short poems as a whole). They are the etched commentaries of an acute observer, or brief lyric meditations.

Much in the above comments might seem to have suggested that Auden is almost always tightly controlled and precise in expression. In parts he is; yet he is just as often large and rhetorical. He likes expressively dramatic flourishes ("The governess in the dead of night / Giving the universe naught for behaviour"—which is a melodramatic image and somewhat cruelly smart). Several of the weaknesses and most of the virtues of his predominant Thirties manner are to be found in the poem *Dover, 1937*:

Steep roads, a tunnel through the downs are the approaches;
A ruined pharos overlooks a constructed bay;
The sea-front is almost elegant; all this show
Has, somewhere inland, a vague and dirty root:
    Nothing is made in this town.

But the dominant Norman castle floodlit at night
And the trains that fume in the station built on the sea
Testify to the interests of its regular life:
Here live the experts on what the soldiers want
    And who the travelers are,

Whom the ships carry in and out between the lighthouses
That guard for ever the made privacy of this bay
Like twin stone dogs opposed on a gentleman's gate:
Within these breakwaters English is spoken; without
    Is the immense improbable atlas.

The eyes of the departing migrants are fixed on the sea,
To conjure their special fates from the impersonal water:
"I see an important decision made on a lake,
An illness, a beard, Arabia found in a bed,
    Nanny defeated, Money."

And filled with the tears of the beaten or calm with fame,
The eyes of the returning thank the historical cliffs:
"The heart has at last ceased to lie, and the clock to accuse;
In the shadow under the yew, at the children's party
    Everything will be explained."

And the old town with its keep and its Georgian houses
Has built its routine upon these unusual moments;
The vows, the tears, the slight emotional signals
Are here eternal and unremarkable gestures
    Like ploughing or soldiers' songs:

Soldiers who swarm in the pubs in their pretty clothes,
As fresh and silly as girls from a high-class academy:
The Lion, the Rose or the Crown will not ask them to die,
Not here, not now. All they are killing is time,
    Their pauper civilian future.

Above them, expensive and lovely as a rich child's toy,
The aeroplanes fly in the new European air,
On the edge of that air that makes England of minor importance;
And the tides warn bronzing bathers of a cooling star,
    With half its history done.

High over France the full moon, cold and exciting
Like one of those dangerous flatterers one meets and loves
When one is very unhappy, returns the human stare:
The night has many recruits; for thousands of pilgrims
The Mecca is coldness of heart.

And the cry of the gulls at dawn is sad like work:
The soldier guards the traveller who pays for the soldier;
Each one prays in the dusk for himself and neither
Controls the years. Some are temporary heroes:
Some of these people are happy.

[*Another Time,* xxvii; *Collected Shorter Poems,* p. 121]

Dover, 1937 is about social and human relations. For Auden the town has unusual interest and significance. As one of our most famous harbours, our representative link with the world outside this island, it sees both endings and beginnings. It is the last point within the territory of "the old gang," and in the Thirties is seen as echoing their seediness, their hollow pretensions and class snobberies. It is also a place from which migrants depart—both those who are trying to run away from themselves (from their psychological problems) and those who seek positively to make a better life; or to which, frustrated or successful, migrants return.

From such a vantage point Auden is able to comment on the condition of Europe and on England's relation to it; on the character of "frontier towns" and on the psychology of migrants (again we meet the Wanderer theme). He can make subsidiary allusions to the human geography of England (Dover is in the South and not industrial; it is, he seems to accuse, parasitic); and to England's social patterns (the soldiery, for instance). He can talk, as so often, about the "lonelies," the frightened souls behind many of our bold personal façades, the sea of individual unhappiness and misery ("Each one prays in the dusk for himself").

Dover, 1937 is able to handle so much matter in so small a space because of the discipline in "objective" writing described above. It can outline detail sharply, pick out the illuminating from the insignificant fact —the soldiers' public-house manners, the architecture of a place which combines seaside-resort-middle-class-country-town-military-centre-and-port. Once the reader is accustomed to the pithy item-by-item strokes of detail and comment and to the concentration of the epithets there are few obscurities. It is a pity that two of the last three stanzas are rather grandly slack; here the addition to large gesture has led to inflation. But the poem recovers in its last verse and ends, as it has been for most of its length, suggestive, rooted in its place and period, epigrammatic and stimulating verse.

The tone is markedly easy and conversational. We are listening to the poet thinking aloud. In the volume of verse which Auden published at the end of this decade (*Another Time*) this conversational manner was predominant. Here Auden owes much to the example of W. B. Yeats, whose conversational verse he has always greatly admired. He has not been able to acquire Yeats's superb facility in this manner (see, for example, Yeats's *Easter, 1916*), but his achievement is not negligible. A short poem, *Musée des Beaux Arts,* might serve well to show the main virtues and weaknesses of this manner as Auden adopts it. With a laconic casualness it makes a searching and moving observation on human suffering, and this is its strength; it is also in parts both knowing and uneasily colloquial.

Even today Auden sometimes writes in a development of this manner, in a relaxed low-temperature verse. This is often what he describes himself as "unofficial poetry." He has always insisted that poetry does not need to be consistently on its high horse; he has always liked to debunk the grand, the "proper," the decorous and the official.

So the Thirties dragged to their grim but honourable conclusion. Like many others—not writers alone—Auden had tried to fight against the trend towards war. It was hard, when war finally broke out, to decide whether their efforts had been rightly directed. Auden had gone on a visit to the United States at the end of 1938 and had remained there. When Germany finally launched her attack on Poland he surveyed from New York the first decade his generation had known as adults. This poem, *1st September, 1939* (written in the metre of Yeats's *Easter, 1916*), sums up the lessons of the experience as he understands them. Its conclusion is religious and so points to the new emphases which were now more and more appearing in Auden's writing. It is obviously the most fitting epilogue to the Thirties as these poets, of whom Auden was the acknowledged leader, had known them.

III. *Lyrics and Songs; Sonnets and Other Forms; Comic Verse*

Auden's technical skill, his poetic virtuosity, is indisputable; he is gifted, professional, a constant practiser. He has more than once said that he is interested in all forms of verse, from the word-of-mouth limerick to the closely designed poem of volume length. He has also said that he opposes all notions of artistic decorum and of "correct" style. So we should expect great range and flexibility in his verse; and we find it. We find also a disposition to play around, just for the fun of it. This occasionally mars the poetry, but not always. It is important not to assume that "playing around" in itself and automatically makes a poem faulty (as though "high seriousness" were indispensable). Auden thinks that the primary characteristic of a budding poet is the wish to "hang around words" and play with them—rather than the wish to reform the world or to become famous. Other professions may give such opportunities; only poetry starts by putting words into odd shapes.

As we move through Auden's poetry we notice a recurrent loyalty to a few forms, as well as a recurrent readiness to experiment. Two forms have obviously attracted him steadily: the brief lyric and the sonnet; we must look further at them later. In his first volume he wrote some curt and gnomic poems which obviously owed something to the poetry of Laura Riding and Robert Graves (*This Lunar Beauty; This One* are two of these). We have discussed the epigrammatic and conversational verse which followed; and in that same period Auden intermittently wrote ballads, choral songs and some poems in little-used forms such as the villanelle, the sestina and the canzone. His comic verse has been fed from several sources: army songs, music-hall and cabaret, jazz. He has from time to time, but notably in *The Age of Anxiety,* modified the alliterative line of Anglo-Saxon poetry. He has been interested in, and has written interestingly about, the challenge presented by opera libretti—the difficulty of writing a clearly running line which can be sung without confusing the singer or the hearer with a complicated interplay of suggestion, and which is yet not simply banal.

These are only typical instances from a wide range of activity by a mind deeply interested in *craft,* in the formal-play element in poetry. In suitable conditions, Auden might well have enjoyed being a court-poet. He would probably have been the court-wit at the same time, but a dry and telling wit—for his "play" usually does have, indirectly, a moral purpose.

When we think of the characteristic texture of Auden's verse we are reminded first of those impersonal and external qualities which were noted earlier. His poems are not strong in some sensory effects. He has a fine ear (as poems such as *Seascape* and *Lullaby* amply show); he responds well to patterns of colour—but seems more interested in the patterns than in the modulations of the colours themselves. There is little touch, taste or smell in his verse. He rarely lingers over his sensory effects—except when they are aural—and seems not greatly interested in them for themselves. We tend to remember his poems as shapes, as patterns of observation and analysis. He once said that he tends to see his own poems as "squares and oblongs"; that is, presumably, as structures formed out of the interplay of man's moral dilemmas. The emphasis is once again on pattern.

Similarly, his epithets do not usually carry rich sensory evocations. Lines such as these, from *Macbeth*:

> Light *thickens;* and the crow
> Makes wing to the *rooky* wood:

would hardly be likely to occur in Auden's poetry. At their most characteristic his epithets do not physically describe the objects they qualify; they are, rather, conceptual. They comment rather than describe; they set the object into a relationship with something or someone else. Often they appear in pairs so that the two adjectives set off an intellectual friction. Auden is likely to say, not "grassy slope," but "tolerant enchanted slope." He does not write:

> Lay your graceful head, my love,
> Golden on my circling arm

but

> Lay your sleeping head, my love,
> Human on my faithless arm

and the interest comes from the play of moral relations between the owners of the head and arm.

Not much need be said about Auden's favourite and recurrent technical habits; nearly all of them are clever but some clever-clever. During the Thirties in particular he made use of a type of simile in which a concrete fact was yoked to an abstract idea. This might produce an effective surprise or might seem merely smart:

> Problems like relatives standing
>
> Will Ferdinand be as fond of a Miranda
> Familiar as a stocking.

He has always been fond of dying falls, especially dying falls with three steps:

> That wept, and grew enormous, and cried Woe.

He has often used a sort of stylized "pointing," by means of successive definite articles:

> The boarding-house food, the boarding-house faces,
> The rain-spoilt picnics in the windswept places,
> The camera lost and the suspicion,

But many of these habits have fallen away during the last few years; today his most frequent excess is in adopting highly unusual words, dictionary-raiding and word-coining.

Auden's lyrics, as we have said, form by now a substantial group within his work and one which can claim considerable admiration. They have some striking common qualities. Most of them create a sense of stillness, the stillness of harmony and calm, or the stillness of menace. They reflect and muse. This is strange, in view of the quick and rather jackdaw-like activity of so much of Auden's poetry. Then one remembers that he quotes more than once—as though it were a reminder and corrective to his own immediate tendencies—Rilke's insistence on the need for a poet to sit still and absorb, to "bless what there is for *being*."

May with its light behaving is a typical Audenesque lyric:

> May with its light behaving
> Stirs vessel, eye and limbs;
> The singular and sad
> Are willing to recover,
> And to the swan-delighting river
> The careless picnics come,
> The living white and red.
> The dead remote and hooded
> In their enclosures rest; but we
> From the vague woods have broken,
> Forests where children meet
> And the white angel-vampires flit;
> We stand with shaded eye,
> The dangerous apple taken.

The real world lies before us,
Animal motions of the young,
The common wish for death,
The pleasured and the haunted;
The dying master sinks tormented
In the admirers' ring;
The unjust walk the earth.
And love that makes impatient
The tortoise and the roe, and lays
The blonde beside the dark,
Urges upon our blood,
Before the evil and the good
How insufficient is
The endearment and the look.
[*Look, Stranger,* xvi; *Collected Shorter Poems,* p. 244]

In spite of the stillness Auden is not, we soon realize, simply absorbing the scene; he is quickly into moral debate again. The allegro opening recalls the pleasure of a May morning, which urges even those held in the grip of their own neuroses to relax, to be happy simply in *being*. This is a moment of simple happiness and gentleness (evoked in part by the interplay of long and short "i" sounds and by the quietly echoing pattern of predominantly off-rhymes or near-rhymes).

Thereafter the poem is sad. We respond to May much as the animals do, at first. But we also stand in the hard light of self-consciousness; we know the doubt of the double-personality, which acts and questions its actions. "Love" prompts us as it prompts "the tortoise and the roe"; but to our self-aware condition "Love" soon shows itself as inadequate. Auden is already moving towards the more complex view of "Love" which he examines in so much of his later work.

The third stanza, with its scraps of psychology, seems far too bitty and overloaded with items; it might have been omitted without much loss. And isn't "vague" in the second stanza (Auden likes the word) so vaguely used as to become an invitation to the reader to supply what suggestions he pleases? By contrast there is an economical charge of meaning in:

The singular and sad
Are *willing* to recover,

and a fine conciseness in:

To the swan-delighting river
The careless picnics come

and in:

> We stand with *shaded* eye
> The dangerous apple taken.

Auden's sonnets are almost always compressed visual or dramatic stories, allegories of some moral problem, tightly held within the fourteen lines and the firm rhyme-scheme. Here again, Rilke is the ancestor. From him Auden learned much about the use of landscape as a symbol for abstract problems otherwise exceptionally difficult to express. "One of the constant problems of the poet," said Auden in a discussion of Rilke, "is how to express abstract ideas in concrete terms." Auden's sonnets often have in common with Rilke's an unannounced jump into the narrative, which forces the reader to pick up the legend as he goes along; a similar air of control; a similar unhurried assurance which comes partly from having firm symbols to manipulate.

Sometimes Auden seems to have become so skilled in this form that he gives the air of producing the sonnets by habit. At such times they have too glossy a finish; he over-works certain movements and phrasings and suggests that his theme has been too easily buttoned-up. Yet at their best the sonnets are good examples of memorable speech. This one shows some of the tricks, but is largely successful:

> So from the years the gifts were showered; each
> Ran off with his at once into his life:
> Bee took the politics that make a hive,
> Fish swam as fish, peach settled into peach.
>
> And were successful at the first endeavour;
> The hour of birth their only time at college,
> They were content with their precocious knowledge,
> And knew their station and were good for ever.
>
> Till finally there came a childish creature
> On whom the years could model any feature,
> And fake with ease a leopard or a dove;
>
> Who by the lightest wind was changed and shaken,
> And looked for truth and was continually mistaken,
> And envied his few friends and chose his love.
> ["In Time of War": 1, *Collected Shorter Poems,* p. 271]

The theme—not in itself unusual—is one which, as we shall see, occurs again and again in Auden. Man is a creature who is forever *becom-*

ing, hardly ever in a state of *being;* he is a double creature, driven by will (free-will *and* wilfulness). The animal and vegetable world (in the octave) simply *is;* without self-consciousness, these things are what they are. Man has freedom to choose, self-consciousness. The poem muses sadly over the weight of consciousness on man but also celebrates it; for man can love, can choose to love and choose when to love. He is bound (bound to choose, even if he chooses not to choose) and free (the way his choice falls depends on him). Hence the close is far more positive than regretful.

IV. *Ideas and Argument; Themes and Development*

We have already noted that Auden went to America in 1938. He stayed there and some years later became an American citizen. His home is in New York, but he has spent much time travelling around America, sometimes teaching for a period at various universities. During the last few years he has kept a small summer home in Europe (first on the Italian island of Ischia and latterly in Austria), in which he may write quietly, away from the stuffy New York summer. In 1956 he was elected Professor of Poetry at the University of Oxford. This post is held for five years, and Auden therefore retired in 1961. During his tenure he spent each summer term (from after Easter to the end of June) in Oxford.

Some critics have said that by breaking his English connections Auden has severed roots essential to the success of his poetry. One can see grounds for such a view: in many of his likes and dislikes, in the peculiar fabric of his feelings (a dry gentleness, a complicated crankly independence, for instance), Auden is recognizably an English writer. Yet the main lines of his thought—and one cannot altogether separate his thought from his own sense of the poetic vocation and so from his poetry—draw upon themes common to all advanced Western societies. In this sense Auden is an unrooted poet, who might equally be at home in any one of the great representative centres of mid-twentieth-century Western life—in Manchester, London, Chicago, Berlin. One may even argue that, given the peculiar temper of his mind, New York—that vast metropolitan mass of "willing" individuals—is his best home, the very symbol of much that lies at the heart of his poetry.

At that heart is a religious view of life, but one almost never withdrawn or mystical. He is, we now know, fascinated by man living on this earth, within societies he has made, fallible but struggling, moving along the tape of time but under the shadow of the timeless reality of God.

We have noted that this was potentially true even in the Thirties, below the immediate political and psychological elements. Auden was never an orthodox Marxist or Freudian. There was always something more. We can follow the way in which this "something more" commands increasing attention by watching his uses of one word, "Love," throughout his poetry. He is often quixotic, but in this shows a remarkably steady development. At the beginning "Love" had a rather undefined and vague meaning ("O Love, the interest itself in thoughtless Heaven"). It yet indicated a quality, both inside man and outside him, which went beyond what either Marxists or Freudians would have recognized. It was disciplined and social, not a self-love; but it was not Christian love. As Auden's thought developed, so this word took on fuller meanings, and eventually he meant by it Christian love, charity, Grace (see *The Prophets*). By then Auden had, of course, become a professed Christian. Of this argument within himself the fullest statement—an argument in couplets—is *New Year Letter,* the book-length poem which appeared in 1941.

Auden has always drawn sustenance from a few selected thinkers, though the thinkers change from time to time. Since the Forties, two of the most influential have been the Danish "existentialist" theologian Søren Kierkegaard (1813-1855) and the living American theologian Reinhold Niebuhr. In Kierkegaard, to take only one instance, he was particularly interested to consider "original anxiety," the basic insecurity of man which reflects his fallen nature and his possible salvation. Much in Niebuhr's thought bears on Auden's interest, not in the mystical, but in the moral dilemmas and social involvements of man living in time and space, held in the fruitful grip of choice, of freedom-with-necessity. These, and many other related themes, occur again and again in Auden's more recent verse. One example, earlier than most but typical, may throw light on the others printed here. This poem is called *Our Bias:*

> The hour-glass whispers to the lion's roar,
> The clock-towers tell the gardens day and night,
> How many errors Time has patience for,
> How wrong they are in being always right.
>
> Yet Time, however loud its chimes or deep,
> However fast its falling torrent flows,
> Has never put one lion off his leap
> Nor shaken the assurance of a rose.

For they, it seems, care only for success:
While we choose words accordindg to their sound
And judge a problem by its awkwardness;

And Time with us was always popular.
When have we not preferred some going round
To going straight to where we are?
[*Another Time,* xv; Penguin Selection, p. 79]

It uses a contrast we have met before. Auden likes to muse over and draw morals from such contrasts. The animals and plants are in a state of simply *being* ("Simply they are," he says elsewhere); man is never perfect or perfectly happy. Presumably no lion has ever looked up and asked itself, "Am I a *good* lion?" let alone, "Am I a *morally* good lion?" Man does this constantly, and Auden reflects on and celebrates the crucial fact—again, in that quiet, almost wry, tone we have noted before. It is compounded of sympathy for man's endless worried muddle, and pride at his energy and his urge to muddle through to something better. We are illogical and messy; for instance, we fall in love with words for their own sakes and refuse to use them simply as conventional signs. If we went straight to our objectives in life, we would not worry about whether the expedient course, the obviously effective course, was also the right course. We would simply follow it. Yet this disposition in itself can hold us back from finding the Truth in God. We can begin to enjoy the Quest, the going round and round, for its own sake. It defers the day of decision, of recognition of our humble and homely duty under God. We are wilful, worrying, maddening—but we choose; and Auden would be one of the last to regret it. He remains humane and purposive; "accept the present in its fulness," he says; work towards building the Just City, even though you know it can never be finally completed.

Until a few years ago, in spite of Auden's efficient professionalism, one was particularly conscious of certain irresolutions in his verse. The four long poems which he wrote soon after settling in America (*New Year Letter, The Sea and the Mirror, For the Time Being* and *The Age of Anxiety*) show much of this difficulty, as do many of the shorter poems written in the years after. He was, for example, often unsure in his tone, affectedly colloquial, showy or overbright; so that one wondered whether his move to America—whatever its grounds—had cut him off from that assurance of a known audience which he would have had if he had remained in Britain.

There were deeper tensions, tensions between Auden the man and Auden the believer, tensions between the believer and the writer. Much of this can be seen in "Prospero to Ariel" and in the long prose speech by Caliban in *The Sea and the Mirror*. "Art is not enough," says Auden more than once. Art—poetry—is interesting and perhaps important; but in what sense is it finally meaningful to the individual soul before God—not only to the individual reader but to the individual creator, the poet himself? It "makes nothing happen." His most typical single phrase from many on this subject is that poetry is "a game of knowledge." It is, first, a game—a form of magic and fun, a release, a playing around; it has fixed rules and needs discipline, but something always depends on luck in the end. Yet it is also in a certain sense concerned with knowledge, and its magic is meaningful. The knowledge is, though, a by-product of the play and comes indirectly, as in the serious absorbed play of a child. In art's harmony and ritual are mirrored the possibility of a greater order outside man's powers. So poetry can help to "direct us to ourselves," can persuade us to a form of "moral rejoicing," can point to "love and truth." At this stage, we realize, we meet the fullest expression of Auden's urge to irradiate human activity with eternal meaning.

The debate is a long and subtle one and not yet completed; it will perhaps never be completed. Auden's latest volume (*Homage to Clio*) suggests that for the moment he is more strongly than ever inclined to think of poetry as "verbal playing," that he is thinking less about what poetry can "do," can reform. He still occasionally writes poems rooted in society (though always seen in relation to God—as in *Friday's Child*). But he often writes poems of quiet religious celebration (*Prime, Precious Five*); or relaxed, playful, elaborate poems.

We have to leave Auden in mid-career. He does not seem likely ever to renounce the writing of poetry altogether, but it may well become increasingly marginal to him. Or he may discover new springs of interest in the writing of poetry. He has at the moment a supple and inscrutable ease in much of his work—like someone amusing himself cleverly on the piano.

Meanwhile, as we look back over the thirty years of his work, we can attempt an interim estimate. He has produced a body of verse which commands our respect and admiration in a number of ways; he has been the brilliant and sometimes profoundly evocative explorer of dilemmas within the human will; in his vividly epigrammatic, conversational and alert verse he held a mirror to a complex decade; he has written a number of lyrics not likely to be soon forgotten. He has been deeply engaged in his time, and has produced some poetry which demands to be judged outside the limitations of that time. He has set an example of devotion to art which few today can equal.

The Poetry of W. H. Auden

by Carlo Izzo

Wystan Hugh Auden was sitting with me at one of the tables of a beerhouse in Venice. I think I can claim a certain familiarity with foreigners (especially English and American ones) and with their languages and countries. And yet I looked at this man, I scrutinized him, and, try as I would, I could not shake off a sense of puzzlement even greater than I usually feel in my relations with other men and women, both common and uncommon, or with literary works, that I have come to know only as an adult—a knowledge not imbibed with my mother's milk, not rooted in the unfathomable soil of the ancestral subconscious. Thus, Giacomo Leopardi is almost a childhood memory—has entered my blood stream through many generations; but Percy Bysshe Shelley is the nebulous enthusiasm I experienced at twenty, when I was enraptured with the magic of a language, seen, as it were, through gauze—a language which was in its own right a precious prize, hard-won, something to be proud of, and, at the same time, something outside me, an obstacle which has never been completely smoothed out.

W. H. Auden presented an enigma harder to solve than these. He is a tall, fair-haired man, with pale eyes, and eyebrows that are almost white; his face is strikingly and variously lined, as with a grid more or less deeply scored; an almost massive man, and yet rangy and loose-jointed. He met me with a broad, welcoming smile, and an ample, sweeping gesture of his hand, the better to shake mine, a gesture which was much more American than English—instinctive mimicry, maybe, after so many years in the United States. For mimicry is not always a sign of weakness: it can be the sign (and this was certainly Auden's

"The Poetry of W. H. Auden" by Carlo Izzo. The first part of this essay is an abridgment of Professor Izzo's introduction to his translation, with notes, of selected poems by Auden: *Poesie di W. H. Auden* (Parma, Italy: Ugo Guanda Editore, 1952). The latter part consists of excerpts from the same author's *Storia della letteratura inglese dalla Restaurazione ai nostri giorni* (Milan, Italy: Nuova Accademia Editrice, 1963). The English translation is by Camilla Roatta. Printed by permission of the author and the publishers.

case) of an alert and ever-ready sensitiveness, a way of getting into step with other people, of being in sympathy with them and understanding them, like the schoolboy in Edgar Allan Poe's *The Purloined Letter* who beat all the other duller-witted little boys at the game of "even and odd" by identifying himself with them till his mind worked like theirs. Even in our walk from the hotel, W. H. Auden strode along with a broad, loping, typically American gait, a gait which was a conquest, not a surrender; and it occurred to me that probably he had already discovered far more about me than I had about him. I simply could not make myself believe that this was the same man who had wielded such almost aggressive influence on his fellow undergraduates at Oxford, who bested them all with the vividness and vigor of his intelligence and culture, with his white-hot reserve, with the cold lucidity of his opinions, and with the high-handed way he had of passing judgment on their weaknesses, on what to him seemed their ill-considered literary preferences or their puking attempts at poetry. One has to read Stephen Spender's *World Within World* to understand what W. H. Auden was in the eyes of the men who were up with him at the University:

> Calling on Auden was a serious business. One made an appointment. If one arrived early one was liable to find the heavy outer door of his room, called the "oak," sported as a sign that he was not to be disturbed. When with him, one was liable to be dismissed suddenly and told the interview was at an end.[1]

And yet, I could see him too in my mind's eye, with his almost albino pigmentation, this night bird blinking in the Venetian summer, as Stephen Spender describes him: sitting in the half-darkness of his small room with the blinds always lowered, dangerously silent, and then suddenly caustic and terse, or again, staring into the void, intoning a kind of soliloquy.

He answered my questions with immediate interest, and seemed sincerely anxious to help me, full of gratefulness, in a perfectly straightforward way, for the attention I was devoting to his poetry. Perhaps he was inclined to be tolerant because I was a foreigner; perhaps, because of this, he was willing to concede that, without being hopelessly obtuse, I might find the going a little difficult; had I been English or American, I suspect he would have taken a different, perhaps an aggressive, tone. But, on the contrary, he never seemed tired of going over the

[1] *World Within World* (London: Hamish Hamilton, 1951), p. 50.

same ground and explaining, even when I kept coming back to the same difficulty with three or four different questions, until I had gone all the way round the point at issue and had tried to throw light on its every facet.

I shall return later to the themes that were discussed when we met and in our correspondence both before and after these encounters. But here, before anything else, I just wanted to give the reader, and not only the reader of today, a human approach. Not today's reader only, because if Auden's work is destined to live, as I believe it is, then it is our duty to show the living man, especially for the benefit of future scholars; they will have, it is true, the immeasurable advantage of knowing the entire body of his work and being able to see it in perspective, but as regards the man himself, they will always have to rely on the judgment of his contemporaries, on our direct experience, on the sensitiveness of our reactions as eyewitnesses—as men suffering from the same ills as he, oppressed by the same problems, finding the courage to go on living in the same hopes.

Taken all in all, the impression Auden makes is most pleasing and convincing: here is a man who is open, genuine, unaffected, truly in love with Poetry (and not just with his own poetry), who can talk about it for hours on end, without showing any signs of tiredness or boredom, for whom poetry is the one passion, the one reality of his life. I told him I was working on Charles Dickens, and it was clear that he shared my enthusiasm for the great Victorian, at whose name so many contemporary intellectuals, including some Englishmen, turn up their noses—people who only enjoy pretentious messed-up *friandises* and are incapable of appreciating a good, strength-giving plate of home-cooked food, or a nice, juicy, underdone steak; bloodless creatures who shudder away from the literary fare they seem to be most in need of. W. H. Auden loves Dickens. Which means that his subtle intelligence tending to abstraction and his rare learning have not blinded him to the worth of a spontaneous genius, sketchily educated, often vulgar, and yet, when the god is upon him, peerless. His devotion to Dante, whom he reads and rereads in the original, must also be recorded—"the flint-faced exile," the poets' poet, for Auden and for T. S. Eliot the greatest of them all.

W. H. Auden is forty-five now [1952], so he was scarcely fifteen when T. S. Eliot published *The Waste Land,* which is the poem of the century, and James Joyce, *Ulysses,* which is the novel of the century. In other words, T. S. Eliot and James Joyce were already a part of contemporary culture when W. H. Auden had not yet taken out nationalization papers for the Republic of Letters. He is a contemporary of Stephen Spender, Cecil Day Lewis, and Louis MacNeice, and so belongs to the generation born in the shadow of W. B. Yeats and T. S. Eliot: the generation, that is to say, that found itself in the position of feeling reverent toward and yet estranged from the former, with his supremely skillful musicality, closer as it is to the senses than to the intellect, while before the latter, with intellectual vigor underpinning all his work, their attitude was one of attention, if not worry, lest sentiment should get the upper hand and slip into sentimentalism. From Dante, his acknowledged and revered master, Eliot has learned above all to seek the geometric locus at which passion and rationality, song and the precepts of philosophy, instinct and awareness of motives, balance each other and find simultaneous expression.

Auden's pre-eminence among the poets of his generation, which is now universally acknowledged, is due particularly to the fact that he turns a deaf ear to the treacherous sirens of nostalgia. Not so Stephen Spender, of whom it is possible to say, "He has a discerning mind, with a delicate awareness, which in another age would have flourished in romantic sensibilities."[2] Not so Cecil Day Lewis, "still fluctuating between a tradition which he distrusts, but in which he is quite at home, and a conviction which his mind applauds but his imagination has not yet fully accepted."[3] Not so Louis MacNeice, who admits explicitly and almost complacently to seeking a conscious and studied modernity: "In examining my own poems I find that, when they are obscure, it is either because my meaning is complicated or because, while having a clear meaning, I consent to compromise its lucid expression for the sake of a gain in speed, concentration, colour, or the music of the verse."[4] Auden alone knows how to translate the inevitable, necessary echoes of tradition into terms which express the constriction of the present age without vain regrets for a past that has been overtaken and submerged by reality. Auden's work reaches forward, not merely conceptually or formally, but lyrically, toward the building of a new literary civilization, while the old grinds away like a wheel without a grip, its premises more like the end of an epoch than a beginning.

[2] B. Ifor Evans, *English Literature Between the Wars* (London: Methuen, 1948), p. 131.

[3] Louis Untermeyer, *Modern American and British Poetry* (New York: Harcourt, Brace & World, Inc., 1942), p. 458.

[4] Louis MacNeice, *Modern Poetry* (London: Oxford University Press, 1938), p. 174.

On the purifying pyre at the end of *Little Gidding,* T. S. Eliot has sacrificed individualism, and his individual self. After the cracked knell of *The Hollow Men* Eliot could find a new birth, a new birth too as a poet, only in religious faith. With the symbol of the mystic rose which concludes *Little Gidding,* he attains a new limit, beyond which it is impossible to go any further in the same direction; nor can one believe that he will again find, as he did when he was forty, the way to a new faith, disclosing other horizons. In the rhetoric of celebrations we may let ourselves be carried away and call poetry "divine," but it is in fact a human phenomenon, of this earth, and after *Little Gidding* it is difficult to see what "earthly" expression Eliot could still find for his mysticism, which denies sensible appearances; certainly *The Cocktail Party* —in which one is tempted to ask where the drawing room ends and the cathedral begins—does not solve the dilemma. The poetry of intellect reaches its conclusion (nor could it be otherwise) in pure abstraction, which is as good as saying in the negation of poetry. So has the Homeric myth of the demigods ended in the everyday, unheroic, uneventful man-in-the-street Bloom—*homo sapiens* scientifically, but with the most exalted artistic mastery, vivisected. In the words of Dante, *"All'alta fantasia qui mancò possa."* [5]

It is not by chance that in English fiction today there is a return to leisurely, traditional story forms. It is an explicit admission that one can travel no further along that road. For Joyce, too, is the end of an era. After Homer, with his superhuman situations perfectly balancing equally superhuman characters; after Shakespeare's unbalance between extraordinary situations and characters of a stature that can face up to them tempestuously, only to be overwhelmed by them in the end; after the Romantic disharmony between passionately violent situations and characters helplessly carried along by them like straws in a flood, Joyce re-establishes an equilibrium, but it is an equilibrium between ordinary, flat, everyday situations, on the one hand, and equally ordinary, flat, everyday characters on the other. "Thus Romanticism," Mario Praz writes, "appears to have reached the end of its evolution: utter impassiveness before the inner world it had itself revealed. Romanticism was born as absolute emotion; it ends as absolute cerebration." [6] The wheel has come full circle: for the higher notes of the scale, the abstraction of mysticism; for the lower ones, the coldness of scientific reasoning. No thoroughfare: "Winter completes an age." We must begin again. After

[5] "High phantasy lost power and here broke off": *Paradiso,* xxxiii, 142; translated by B. Reynolds.

[6] Mario Praz, *Storia della letteratura inglese,* 6th ed. (Florence: Sansoni, 1951), p. 386.

the early Middle Ages with their skeleton ruins, the later Middle Ages achieved the great rebirth, which was to wither again, though sumptuously, into a return to the past, first set in motion by Humanism. Now the Middle Ages have again descended on humanity, after the breakdown of the tawdry ideals proclaimed by the nineteenth century, and now surely it is time for the cycle to start again. How and where this will happen, it is difficult to foretell. Certainly the way will not be opened by the well-constructed novel of events set down in chronological order, in accordance with the nineteenth-century pattern, of which it appears there is a revival in England, following on the rediscovery of Anthony Trollope in the war years. This cannot be a starting point for the future development of English fiction: James Joyce can be renounced but not ignored. The same applies to poetry. After T. S. Eliot one cannot go back *sic et simpliciter* to full-throated song, not even to that of William Butler Yeats. Nor can we be content with the self-conscious, doctrinaire modernness of poets who have their eyes turned to the future, but whose hearts often seem exiled in some provincial backwater, so that one can fancy them singing:

> I have left my heart behind
> In an old cathedral town. . . .

But to return to W. H. Auden, here is a poet who really lives in his own time, post-Eliot, post-Joyce, and lives in it with the whole man, brain and heart, bag and baggage. Hence his right to be considered the most representative of his contemporaries. Even the fact that he has both English qualities (because he was born and bred in England and went to an English university) and American ones (because he has chosen to become a citizen of the United States, thus reversing T. S. Eliot's itinerary), seems to mark him out for the particular attention of students of current Anglo-American literature. For, since Pound, the two sundered halves of English-language literature (and especially of lyric poetry, which is less influenced by the day-to-day impact of life and local customs) seem to be on the way to joining up once more and settling down to the symbiosis which was so rudely interrupted by Whitman's secession. Nowadays, a tang too sharply American has something old-fashioned and provincial about it. W. H. Auden, with his dual nationality, is already to some extent a citizen of the world, a forerunner of tomorrow's more concerted song.

"As to my excessive talent, at an early stage the demon, who never gives without taking, raised a formidable objection. Since then I have never been able to accomplish anything without its being counter-balanced by some disappointment. Innocence is something I have had to acquire." In these words from his book *Prologhi,* Vincenzo Cardarelli identifies and indirectly defines an artist's most insidious enemy: an excess of talent resulting in an incapacity for innocence. In Bernard Shaw, for instance, there was an excess of dialectic subtlety, there was his acrobatic, not to say diabolical, skill in upholding with equal brilliance and persuasiveness opposite points of view. In Gabriele D'Annunzio there was an excess of verbal richness and luxuriance of expression; the *"Imaginifico"* (Wizard of Words, Spinner of Conceits), as Alfredo Panzini called him, was cursed with the Midas touch. But W. H. Auden has to excess the power of association: the frequent strangeness of his metaphors, the cunning richness of his use of adjectives, the agility of his epigrams, the audacity and swiftness of his foreshortened images, hints that are vivid and yet cryptic—all these create a dazzle on the surface of his speech through which it is often difficult to perceive the outline, shape, and lyrical substance lying beyond or under the words, which, instead of being tools, take the stage as protagonists. It is like witnessing a play in which the gorgeousness of the costumes or the over-weening exhibitionism of some actor make us lose sight of the gist of the actual drama itself. Of course, it is true that a lyric poem is, as Massimo Bontempelli put it, "an adventure in words"; but just as there are characters who get the upper hand of a novelist or playwright, there can be words or tricks of style that get the upper hand of a poet.

Hoggart stresses the influence of Rainer Maria Rilke on Auden's poetics: "There is the same clear symbolisation in landscape and incident of abstract problems otherwise difficult to express; the same unheralded jump into the narrative which requires the reader to pick up the legend as he goes along." [7] That Rilke's influence on the whole of contemporary poetry has been considerable is a critical proposition which does not need confirming; it is significant that the English translations of his work sometimes have a tone very close to Auden's. It must be borne in mind, however, that contemporary poetry indulges in the use and abuse of symbols, "objective correlatives," drawn from relatively unexplored recesses of ethnology, psychoanalysis, rare and neglected

[7] Richard Hoggart, *Auden: An Introductory Essay* (London: Chatto and Windus, 1951), pp. 42-43.

branches of learning, and private experience; it is very probable that if one were to submit to the same reader poems he didn't know by Yeats, Eliot, and Auden, mixed with English translations of Paul Valéry, Rainer Maria Rilke, and, from Italy, of Eugenio Montale, that reader would be seriously put to it to sort out the authorship of the various specimens. It has always been like that: poets of a generation have a family air. In a hundred years' time everyone will be able to distinguish between spiritual affinity, unconscious imitation, and plagiarism and will think themselves (quite wrongly) so much cleverer than we are, but we as yet are too close to the poetry of our time to see it stereoscopically.

Here is an instance of what I mean: in "Prime," the first poem in *Nones,* these lines occur:

> Recalled from the shades to be a seeing being,
> From absence to be on display,
> Without a name or history I wake
> Between my body and the day.

Well, it is not in the slightest degree necessary for Auden to be acquainted with "Aurore," nor yet with "Air de Sémiramis," by Paul Valéry, nor to have had a conscious or unconscious recollection of them, while writing these lines, in order to explain the analogy with

> *La confusion morose*
> *Qui me servait de sommeil,*
> *Se dissipe dès la rose*
> *Apparence du soleil.*
>
> *A peine sorti des sables,*
> *Je fais des pas admirables*
> *Dans les pas de ma raison*
>
> ["Aurore"]

or with

> *Dès l'aube, chers rayons, mon front songe a vous ceindre!*
> *A peine il se redresse, il voit d'un oeil qui dort*
> *Sur le marbre absolu, le temps pâle se peindre. . . .*
>
> *. . . Sois enfin toi-même, dit l'Aurore,*
> *O grande àme, il est temps que tu formes un corps.*
> ["Air de Sémiramis"]

"A family likeness." And how much in the manner of Paul Valéry is a line like "Between my body and the day" ("Palme": *"Entre l'ombre et le soleil; Entre le sable et le ciel"*), or the very special use of the word *absence* (so written in French, too), an entirely subjective musical impression, which transcends rational, objectively critical comparisons such as can be expressed in words. In this particular case, however, there is an inescapable consideration which is wholly to the advantage of the French poet. Paul Valéry does not resort to startling metaphors such as Auden's "Between my body and the day," a line which, in spite of its luminous beauty, *is* startling. He confines himself to apparently obvious statements and, in speaking of a palm, is almost trite: "Between the shadow and the sun; Between the sand and the sky." And yet—by the alchemy that occurs when a magician touches the Word with his philosopher's stone—he manages to place these phrases apart in an atmosphere so clean and still and enchanted that the most ordinary words, which in any other context would have no evocative power whatever, seem new-minted, wet with the morning dew, like the earliest-known poetic fragments.

There is no doubt that in Auden's "excess of talent" we must also include his amazing powers of assimilation. In his youthful period, Wordsworth; then T. S. Eliot, W. B. Yeats, Hardy, Gerard Manley Hopkins, Wilfred Owen; and besides these, Anglo-Saxon poetry, Langland and John Skelton; then Dryden, Pope, Samuel Butler (the author of *Hudibras*), Byron, William Blake, Browning, and, in some of the prose passages in his plays, Henry James; also, among foreign writers, Rainer Maria Rilke and Kafka; and Emily Dickinson; and, among modern writers, besides those already mentioned, Edward Thomas, Robert Graves, Laura Riding; and finally, as we have seen, Paul Valéry (not quoted by other critics, to my knowledge). So many are the names and often so unconcealed the derivations, that we must consider this spongelike quality of Auden's an essential part of his personality. To call him a chameleon or, worse still, to talk of mystification would be in the highest degree foolish and unjust. The unity of his inspiration is in no way impaired by these echoes, which should be considered, rather, as symptoms of his untameable restlessness and urge to experiment; for Auden is always reaching forward and attempting new paths—until at last he finds one that leads him to the highway of truth, which is the same for everybody and also different for everybody, according to the form given to it by each of us according to his nature. In any case, owing to the vastness of Auden's culture, it would be extremely difficult to establish, every time we find an echo, whether it is merely a coincidence, a conscious or an unconscious derivation, or an intentional allusion. For instance, take the lines

> And look, behind you without a sound
> The woods have come up and are standing round
> In deadly crescent,

from the poem "The Witnesses": are they an unconscious reminiscence of Birnam Wood in *Macbeth,* or a deliberate allusion to it? And take the beginning of "The Labyrinth": "*Anthropos apteros* for days"; is it a somewhat faint echo of Ezra Pound, or is it merely "the family likeness"?

Though we must acknowledge that Auden's spiritual position, even now, after his conversion, is closer to earthly problems than T. S. Eliot's, the latter's influence on Auden the playwright would seem to be incontrovertible: it runs all through the plays, from those written in collaboration with Christopher Isherwood during his near-Marxist period to the most recent ones, and includes particularly *The Age of Anxiety,* in which the alternation of prose with intensely lyrical or violently elliptical passages is obviously typical of Eliot. At first the influence was only on the style, but now, as a consequence of their points of view drawing nearer to each other, it has become conceptual as well, as in "The Sea and the Mirror," in which the admonition

> But we have only to learn to sit still

echoes the line

> Teach us to sit still

used by Eliot as the last-but-third of the first part of *Ash Wednesday,* and then again toward the end of the sixth and last part, almost like a refrain which holds the series of poems together, and whose spirit seeps through them all.

One does not approach a contemporary poet who is still young, still fully active, and experiencing a continual process of renewal, with the aspiration or illusion of passing a definitive judgment on him, not even so far as his already published work is concerned. In the particular case of the singularly prismatic and restless Auden, not only would an attempt at a comprehensive summing up be rash, but even the most cautious critical anticipation would be fraught with danger. He is contemporary in a spiritual, not merely in a historical, sense; he fits the times like a glove, and his thought seeps into and follows every curve and inlet of the twentieth-century mind and conscience; this makes him the most distinguished, but also the most fluid, poet of his generation and the most difficult personality to pin down within a formula.

The dilemmas and, when they are not actually contradictory, the alternatives of our age are W. H. Auden's deeply probed and deeply felt themes. The age is divided: on the one hand, conquests of the mind and, undeniably, of science; on the other, a painful nostalgia for spiritual belief. So also is W. H. Auden divided between his pitilessly critical intellect and a need, consciously felt, for a world less diseased and stricken with wrongs, mistrust, terror. While a further dichotomy splits the age between its quest for a new faith and an irony which has seldom been as corrosive at any other time in history, there is similarly a split in Auden between the temptation he feels to run for shelter "howling to his art" as though to a fortress, and the consciousness that his art ("Voltaire at Ferney"; "In Memory of W. B. Yeats") has a mission to accomplish from which he has not the right to withdraw. The age is eroded by reason's mistrust of sentiment and sentiment's mistrust of reason, and Auden would like to be able to let himself go and express himself straightforwardly in a way more accessible to the many, and yet not always can he resist the blandishments of his imagination with its excessive brilliance and captiousness—that "excess of talent" which inveigles him into being more esoteric and involved than he wishes. Anxiously, feverishly, this age of ours is trying to find a voice of its own, torn between the death of the individual, desperately trying to fight death off, and the first faint cries of a new feeling of brotherhood, transcending the individual but still in its infancy; anxiously, Auden tries to reconcile the demands of a juster society with the Christian conception of resignation and forgiveness. Yes, it is difficult as yet to spike him like a butterfly on a pin.

More difficult than ever after his last [as of 1952] book of verse, *Nones,* and after my even more recent personal contact with him; on that occasion his insistence that certain of his technical devices should not be sacrificed in translation revealed to me that he considers—or has come to consider once more—his incomparable skill in versification of primary importance in the general economy of his work. It is a pregnant discovery. It leads one to suspect that the various "subjects" and "manners" which can be traced in Auden's work have been chiefly "pretexts" for him to exercise his "excessive talent," and give full vent, to the point of exhaustion, to his almost unlimited versatility. It is Ezra Pound's lesson: when you have nothing essential to say stored up inside, instead of chewing the cud of your minor infatuations, or caroling about the flowers that bloom in the spring tra-la, it is much better to experiment with new forms of expression. If the experiment is, or seems to be, successful, obviously it will be important in the eyes of the experimenter, and, equally obviously, he will want the reader to perceive this importance too; the reader, after all, has not the right to expect a masterpiece at every page. So Auden's near-Marxist period, and that of his first enthusiam for the "idea of a Christian society," during both of which his concern with technique seemed to take second place compared to the urgency of the "message" to be communicated and the necessity of making it abundantly intelligible, were periods in which the poet "had something essential stored up" and in which his feeling was at its most fervent, if not at its most profound. His up-to-date awareness might also resolve itself into a fluid adaptability, so that everyday experience, pushing and knocking, would rub against the faculties of association and expression and cause the spark (never mind how fleeting) indispensable to poetic creation. Therefore the Freudian experience, filtered through some of the master's more recherché and subtle followers such as Prinzhorn, Klages, Groddeck; the philosophy of Kierkegaard; the ideas of Pascal, Goethe, Nietzsche; the theories of Homer Lane on education; the Freudian offshoots in the works of D. H. Lawrence; in addition to the varied stylistic experiences we have spoken of, down to the present Eliotish orientation —these may be, ultimately, nothing but the armature on which the sculptor, calling upon the resources of his technique and his motives, *seeks* and finally models *his* statue. To sum up, I would distinguish at least four different elements in Auden's work: the contribution of his cultural and literary experiences, which have only an external impact and don't touch the heart of the matter; his quick responsiveness to contingent reality, from Marxism to disappointment in it and to his present withdrawal to a particular brand of Christianity, in which he endeavors to reconcile the individual demands of his own spiritual salvation with universal salvation based on fraternity and justice for all; the "laboratory research" showily apparent in his youth, almost completely abandoned in the near-Marxist period and in the years of his Christian (or may it be his *near*-Christian?) novitiate, but latterly returned to a place of honor; and finally—and this is the constant theme that runs through all his apparently different incarnations—the drama of the contemporary artist, of the "double man" oscillating insecurely between the attraction of Art for Art's sake and the conviction that art is a mere game and irrelevant to the culminating moments in history, between Marxist determinism and the aspiration to "freedom in necessity," between a (negative) loathing for love as it is generally conceived and a (positive) eagerness that it should become a love of mankind.

Not for nothing was his *New Year Letter* (1940), which was a turning point in contemporary English literary history, called *The Double Man* in the original American edition, a title far closer to the spirit of the book. It was later taken up by Spender—in the form, as we have seen, of *World Within World,* but with the same meaning—for his autobiography, and Auden himself has returned to it in *The Enchafèd Flood, or The Romantic Iconography of the Sea* (1951), in which are collected a series of three most remarkable lectures on the symbology of the sea in world literature, from its origins to the present day. In this work Auden speaks of "the double-natured hero, half Bedouin, i.e. Ishmael, the exile, the Wandering Jew, the Flying Dutchman, and half Don Quixote, i.e. the dedicated man, the Knight of Faith who would restore the Age of Gold."

The Double Man (or *New Year Letter*) was the announcement of a conversion. However, of the "two" men, the one to be converted looms considerably larger than the converted one. Evidence of this is the intellectual Satanism with which the poem is imbued from start to finish: scintillating with corrosive irony, overflowing with mockery and contempt, the author complacently surveys his own almost unbelievable verbal agility. The meter, lifted whole from Samuel Butler's *Hudibras,* is the visible sign of an attitude of mind which justifies the coupling of Auden's name with Byron's (and, as a contrast, of Spender's with Shelley's). But in Auden there is a capacity for faith without rhetoric which was lacking in the author of *Don Juan.* Satire bursts forth in him as a positive element of renewal, not as a merely negative condemnation of the contemporary world from which he announces his secession:

> . . . the heart,
> As Zola said, must always start
> The day by swallowing its toad
> Of failure and disgust.

So begins the last part of the poem. Having spat out all the bile in his system—or "swallowed his toad"—the poet moves on to his catharsis.

In the volumes of verse published after *Nones,* namely *The Shield of Achilles* (1955) and *Homage to Clio* (1960), Auden's attitude is no longer the polemical one which he had assumed around 1938 together with Stephen Spender and Cecil Day Lewis (and of which a clear instance is the poem "A Communist to Others"), nor the attitude of "anxiety" or of barely stirring hope of the following period, up to and after 1945; he now treads the solid ground of his convictions, under a sky which is clear again, following an itinerary not unlike that of T. S. Eliot. Although in the dedicatory quatrain of *The Shield of Achilles* he shows himself to be aware that we live in "bad lands, where eggs are small and dear" and that we seem to be traveling "by a stonier Track" toward worse experiences, nevertheless, he says, it is when all are spent that there will arise "the right song—for the wrong time of year." There follows in the epigraph to the second part of the book the invocation:

> Guard, Civility, with guns
> Your moods and your declensions;
> Any lout can spear with ease
> Singular Archimedes.

In one of the poems of this second part the poet's new orientation is confirmed, not only by what he wittily says, but by the rhythmic structure he has chosen. The poem is in rhymed couplets of five-foot iambics (the meter of John Dryden and Alexander Pope), and its title is "The Truest Poetry is the Most Feigning"; both by its subject and its form it represents the ultimate extreme of refinement and "civility." The subject is summed up in the opening lines:

> By all means sing of love but, if you do,
> Please make a rare old proper hullabaloo:
> When ladies ask How much do you love me?
> The Christian answer is *così-così:*
> But poets are not celibate divines;
> Had Dante said so, who would read his lines?
> Be subtle, various, ornamental, clever . . .
> Good poets have a weakness for bad puns.

"Horae Canonicae," the third part of the book, culminates in the poem "Sext." The gifts which are supposed to have come to us from "civility" are here exalted to the point that civility is credited with having staged the trial of Christ (made possible because civilization was socially organized) and of having nailed Christ to the cross—thus opening the way for what the poet, whose youth, like Eliot's, was spent far from religious belief, or at any rate in ignorance of it, now considers the redemption of mankind. The lyric begins by praising men capable of "forgetting themselves in a function," and adds:

> There should be monuments, there should be odes,
>
> to the first flaker of flints
> who forgot his dinner,
>
> the first collector of sea-shells
> to remain celibate.

In Auden the ability to translate concept into episode or image is always limpid and exquisite; as here in the flaker of flints and the collector of sea-shells.

The theme reappears, borne on the wings of a stronger lyrical impulse, in the poem (from the same book) entitled "Streams."

In *Homage to Clio* a new note rings out: the other goddesses can be portrayed, says Auden, in sculpture or in painting:

> . . . but what icon
> Have the arts for you, who look like any
>
> Girl one has not noticed and show no special
> Affinity with a beast? I have seen
> Your photo, I think, in the papers, nursing
> A baby or mourning a corpse: each time
>
> You had nothing to say and did not, one could see,
> Observe where you were, Muse of the unique
> Historical fact, defending with silence
> Some world of your beholding, a silence
> No explosion can conquer but a lover's Yes
> Has been known to fill. . . .

. . . Approachable as you seem,
I dare not ask you if you bless the poets,
For you do not look as though you ever read them
Nor can I see a reason why you should.

The "lover's Yes," filling and overpowering Clio's silence (and really the Muse seems more like a witness of human anguish than its architect), is without precedent in Auden's work; but he has always had amazing powers of renewal.

The theme is taken up again, in a markedly subjective key, in "Walks." In accordance with the metaphorical process which is customary in Auden and is his most remarkable contribution to twentieth-century English poetry (though the roots of the method are to be found in the metaphysical poets), the idea to be expressed is translated into concrete, or apparently concrete, terms. When, Auden says, I have to go to a particular place on a particular errand, I take the same road coming back that I took going, because "the road looks altogether new / Now that is done I meant to do." But when I go for a walk just for the exercise, without a particular aim, I follow a circular route. Otherwise the fact of having to turn back at some point would create problems I could never solve:

What good or evil angel bid
Me stop exactly when I did?
What would have happened had I gone
A kilometre further on?

But this is not all: the poet also wants a hundred yards of path all his own, connecting his house with the public highways, both the straight and the curving one, so that the plan of the straight walk will be like a "T" and that of the circular walk like a "Q." Clever and clear. But what is surprising is the motive for this private path: it is a byway no other traveler uses, so that, if the poet should find footprints on it which do not fit his own shoes, he will know the footprints "have looked for me and, like enough / Were made by someone whom I love." Not, you notice, "Who loves *me*," but "Whom *I* love." What matters is the love we give, not the love we receive. W. H. Auden has come a long journey—from love of the community to despondency, from despondency to transcendental faith, from transcendental faith to a too-complacent preoccupation with technical devices; and, at the end, it would seem that the poet has found, or found again, the love of man: no longer of man as the anonymous community, but of man as an individual. Perhaps to love the community truly one must see in it not just one anonymous face but many faces, each one different, and in each recognize a brother. This would seem to be the road that Auden is signposting for us today: a difficult one, perhaps, to travel on to the end, but certainly the noblest that man can undertake, torn as he is between the cult of his private self and the duties that are his lot as a member of the community.

No wonder Auden's poetry has had imitators and that the youngest men writing today regard themselves as his followers, if not disciples, or at least as his companions. It is not a question of greatness, nor of the likelihood of permanent fame. Playing the prophet is an idle pastime. It is not the future that is the question here, but the present, and what we have in Auden is an extraordinary perceptiveness of the present and complete command of the right language to express it. The combination cannot fail to attract whoever is trying to find an answer to the problems of today in terms of today, or whoever wants to see yesterday's myth put on leaves again in a new interpretation. The latter is the case of the poem in *The Shield of Achilles* that gives its name to the book:

> That girls are raped, that two boys knife a third,
> Were axioms to him, who'd never heard
> Of any world where promises were kept,
> Or one could weep because another wept.

This sounds not so much like scenes on Achilles' shield as like some of the problems that tragically afflict today's society. Only in the light of a mind like Auden's, which, at the same time, gives out brightness and is itself enlightened, can today's society see itself reflected with all the flaws that may rupture it and find the way to redemption out of the blind alley in which it seems to have lost itself.

The Sea and the Mirror

by Frederick P. W. McDowell

"The Sea and the Mirror" in scope and beauty is, as some critics have maintained, Auden's masterpiece.[1] Tautly organized, its components balance and interweave with one another. The pleasure to be had from the whole supplements, in the Coleridgean sense, the pleasure to be had from its parts. The Stage Manager's short prologue parallels Ariel's brief epilogue spoken to Caliban; Caliban's earthy but involuted prose address to the audience complements Prospero's dignified and colloquial address to Ariel; and the short speeches of the other characters collected under "The Supporting Cast, Sotto Voce" are enclosed in the center of the poem. These people form not only the pivot of psychological interest but are centrally located so as to seem accessible to the influences acting upon them from outside, notably those of Prospero, Ariel, and Caliban.

The Stage Manager asserts that the abstractions of the logical mind are not the full truth and that intangible values, which supplement those given us by the intellect, exist:

> Well, who in his own backyard
> Has not opened his heart to the smiling
> Secret he cannot quote?
> Which goes to show that the Bard

"The Sea and the Mirror." Excerpted, with the author's consent, from "'The Situation of Our Time': Auden in His American Phase" by Frederick P. W. McDowell, in *Aspects of American Poetry: Essays Presented to Howard Mumford Jones* (Columbus: Ohio State University Press, 1962) edited by Richard M. Ludwig, pp. 223-55. The excerpt reprinted here constitutes the concluding section (pp. 243-55) of Professor McDowell's essay.

[1] Mark Schorer, "Auden, Shakespeare and Jehovah," *New York Times Book Review* (September 17, 1944), p. 4; Francis Scarfe, *W. H. Auden* (Monaco, 1949), p. 49; Edward Callan, "The Development of W. H. Auden's Poetic Theory since 1940," *Twentieth Century Literature,* IV (October, 1958), 84; and Bent Sunesen, "'All We Are Not Stares Back at What We Are': A Note on Auden," *English Studies,* XL (December, 1959), 439-49.

Was sober when he wrote
That this world of fact we love
Is unsubstantial stuff:
All the rest is silence
On the other side of the wall;
And the silence ripeness,
And the ripeness all.

This passage reveals Auden's skill in making fresh poetry from familiar Shakespearean phrases. The last four lines, moreover, convey an acceptance and a reconciliation, linked with Ariel's wisdom in the postscript. There Ariel, who is the artistic impulse in essence, wants Caliban as he is, and welcomes "reality," epitomized in Caliban, no matter how gross or grotesque. The ripeness is all, both for Ariel who welcomes Caliban's "drab mortality" and for Caliban who, in his long prose speech, disparages the production he has just witnessed and by implication the whole human performance, but who still perceives through it intimations of the "Wholly Other Life."

"Prospero to Ariel," the first section, is Audenesque in its easy but sinewy style, its colloquial charm, and its vigor of idiom. The naturalness of diction and rhythm in these lines combines with a dignity of tone appropriate to Prospero's dedication as artist and with an intellectuality which supports the closely reasoned aspect of his ideas:

Stay with me, Ariel, while I pack, and with your first free act
 Delight my leaving; share my resigning thoughts
As you have served my revelling wishes; then, brave spirit,
 Ages to you of song and daring, and to me
Briefly Milan, then earth.

Auden describes the meter for this speech as couplets with thirteen syllables in the first line, eleven syllables in the second, and consecutive vowel sounds elided.[2] His accomplishment is not only to write well in a constricted meter but to achieve in it a spontaneous rather than a studied effect.

Upon leaving his isle, Prospero is concerned with his double destiny as retired artist and emergent human being. As an old man he now wishes to recover his humanity, somewhat aborted by his excessive concern with art and study; but he is also reluctant to give over his magician's reputation. If art introduces us to an ideal realm of order ("godlike in

[2] Letter from Malcolm Cowley, *Poetry*, LXV (March, 1945), 345.

its permanence and beauty, providing a picture of life which is worthy of imitation of far as it is possible"),[3] it may prevent us from acquiring knowledge of undistorted reality. Art may not only bring out latent values for the maker and the percipient, but it may corrupt the uncritical maker by encouraging moral expediency and the uncritical percipient by suggesting that the harmonies of art are easily attained in life and sufficient to regulate it. Prospero has thus been led by Ariel to forget the two promises he had made as an apprentice: "To hate nothing and to ask nothing for its love." There is Antonio, whom Prospero, by his intellectual withdrawal, encouraged in evil and then could not help hating; and there is Caliban, whom Prospero molded so as to enjoy the satisfaction deriving from the "absolute devotion" of a created object. The failure with Caliban is particularly disturbing, for it undermines Prospero's achievement with the other characters and his spiritual confidence: "his wreck/ That sprawls in the weeds and will not be repaired:/ My dignity discouraged by a pupil's curse,/ I shall go knowing and incompetent into my grave." A further irony is that Prospero is blind to what he needs for a completed wisdom, the refractory realities present in Caliban whom he symbolically rejects by leaving him behind on the isle. The rejection of Caliban is fateful for Prospero because he evades the truth about himself, because he will not recognize the ugly and grotesque, and because he lacks the imagination to understand a sinister being he has himself in part engendered. In the Kierkegaardian sense, Prospero has insight at the aesthetic and moral levels, but lacks insight at the religious. Intellectually to be admired, Prospero in Auden's view lacks the radical charity—or Agape—discernible at times even in reprobates like Falstaff: "Agape requires that we love our enemies, do good to those that hate us, and forgive those who injure us, and this command is unconditional." [4] The formidable Prospero pays lip service to Agape, but does not "unconditionally" embrace it. As Auden says in another connection, "Prospero's forgiving is more the contemptuous pardon of a man who knows he has his enemies completely at his mercy than a heartfelt reconciliation." [5]

Still Prospero has been able to change for the better the attitudes of

[3] "The Dyer's Hand: Poetry and the Poetic Process," *Anchor Review: Number Two* (New York, 1957), p. 257.

[4] "The Fallen City: Some Reflections on Shakespeare's 'Henry IV,' " *Encounter,* XIII (November, 1959), 28.

[5] "Balaam and the Ass: On the Literary Use of the Master-Servant Relationship," *Encounter,* III (July, 1954), 45.

the remaining characters. The exaltation and harmonizing power, common to art and religion, can work positively on people nearer to the normal manifestations of conscience than are Antonio and Caliban. The people on board the ship returning to Milan have "been soundly hunted/ By their own devils into their human selves." With a creator's satisfaction, Prospero views the lovers Ferdinand and Miranda whose "eyes are big and blue with love; its lighting/ Makes even us look new." Possibly their love is too much like the harmonies to be found only in art and too little like the actuality. He wonders what may happen when Miranda becomes to Ferdinand "familiar as a stocking." For himself Prospero is glad to have got beyond the possibility of a disillusioned awakening from the dream of romantic love. At the same time he may have become too subtly corrupted by pride and egotism to experience with abandon the ecstasy of selfless passion.

As for the other chief philosopher in the work, Caliban, his opinions on similar subjects are extensions of Prospero's own. Auden conceived Caliban's address as a virtuoso piece, exploiting Jamesean involutions of syntax to secure added nuances of meaning. From our knowledge of *The Tempest,* it represents a comic reversal of expectation for the slave to be an even more subtle philosopher than the master and a more suave man of the world. It is also the proud Prospero's just fate to be surpassed in insight and sophistication by a contemned underling. It is an added irony that no one, except Caliban himself and his audience, recognizes his superiority. Since in their different realms they are both intrepid, it is not fortuitous that Caliban's conclusions resemble Prospero's. Both agree that the world of art is several removes from the real world. As Caliban says, it presents us with "the perfectly tidiable piece of disorder" but only that. In life something always resists being tidied up: in the second section ("Supporting Cast") the demonic Antonio thus refuses to be reconciled with the spiritual Prospero, and Sebastian's repentance, though real, has been due to accident. Caliban himself is a discordant entity in an artist's universe, except for the artist who has made an honest endeavor to assimilate Caliban's reality. Still, almost all art represents an attempt to reconcile the real and the ideal ("the sounded note is the restored relation"); and we ignore at our peril what art can teach us. In his monologue Caliban describes two types of people who falsify experience by denying the harmonies between the tangible and the intangible to be found in art. There are those who slavishly follow himself and deny Ariel, and those who are lifted to Ariel's rarefied atmosphere and deny the gross reality embodied in himself. Art has a complex and subtle relationship to life; in itself, it can neither be accepted nor rejected as a guide to experience.

The middle section of the poem entitled "The Supporting Cast, Sotto Voce" reveals Auden's virtuosity and insight at their most complex and steady. The form Auden uses for each speaker is appropriate, either directly reflecting the speaker's qualities or providing an ironic commentary upon them. As in Prospero's and Caliban's discourses, form and substance are inseparable.

Antonio dominates this part of "The Sea and the Mirror," in some respects the poem as a whole, because he is the unreconciled figure who threatens to undermine the hard-won peace of the other characters. To convey the involutions of his hatred for Prospero and for the light, Antonio sullenly meditates in the elaborate pattern of *terza rima*. Antonio will prevent Prospero from attaining, first, pure "Being" and, secondly, a perfect grouping of human beings, whereby the harmonies of art might be approximated in life. Antonio's is the motiveless malignity in the background that bides its time to destroy because it must. Antonio will constantly threaten the serenity of Prospero and tempt him to resurrect the wand he has broken and the books he has destroyed. Antonio, evil as he is, has the positive function of checking the pride of Prospero, insidious because of its very benignancy. Antonio's appended comments to each of the speeches in Part II imply that he exists as a challenge in the spiritual lives of his fellows, all the more sinister because no one pierces beneath his appearance to see him as he is. He is a figure no one reckons with until his influence is perhaps disastrously entrenched. In toughness of fiber and strength of purpose he equals Prospero; and just as he formerly wrenched the dukedom from his brother, Antonio is only waiting his opportunity to destroy and humiliate his brother spiritually.

The soliloquies of the other members of the supporting cast also reveal an organic union of idea and form. Thus Ferdinand in the intricate pattern of the sonnet struggles to express his deep but tangled emotions, to crystallize depths of feeling almost inexpressible in words. Subject to the limitations imposed by the sonnet, the welter of his inner being is at last ordered to the point that he can define in the concluding line what Miranda means to him: "The Right Required Time, The Real Right Place, O Light." The hedonist and sensualist, Stephano, speaks through the ballade: the elaborate metrical pattern is in satiric contrast with the plainness and crudeness of his emotions. He finds it difficult to achieve identity apart from his mother; despite his simplicity, his quest is the same as that of his peers: "A lost thing looks for a lost name." The couplet conveying the befuddlement of Adrian and Francisco is engaging nonsense and its brevity a comment upon their vacuity of mind: "Good little sunbeams must learn to fly,/ But it's madly ungay when the goldfish die." For the lyrical expression of simple emotion the master and the boatswain use the popular ballad meter modified into a six-line stanza. As in Stephano's ballade, a universal theme is established, despite the ignorance of the speakers: the isolation of each individual. Describing their liaisons, they not only define their own loneliness but that of the rest: "And two by two like cat and mouse/ The homeless played at keeping house." Trinculo is no intellectual, but his perceptions are more complex than those of the master and boatswain. Accordingly, a form more complex than theirs is necessary, but one not too complicated. Auden therefore assigns him quatrains in iambic trimeter with lines two and four rhyming. Like the master and boatswain, Trinculo knows the overwhelming isolation expressed by the other characters when they are honest with themselves. Trinculo perceives that the clown, like the artist, is subject to fits of "fine frenzy" and to terrors which do not strengthen him spiritually but which do provide him with materials for sardonic humor whereby he can entertain others.

Gonzalo's address in rhyming trochaic tetrameter is well adapted to weighty ideas. In the service of the intellect, he had denied the mystery of being and the provenance of the contingent and the absurd. He is now restored in spirit, has overcome "doubt and insufficient love," and admits the all-importance of a transcendent reality. His opening lines convey the grave beauty and solemnity of his discourse as a whole:

> Evening, grave, immense, and clear,
> Overlooks our ship whose wake
> Lingers undistorted on
> Sea and silence.

In Gonzalo's speech Auden reveals his marked ability to modulate the moods of his characters. Sobriety yields by degrees to subdued rejoicing as Gonzalo in the last stanza accepts with humility his deliverance:

> Even rusting flesh can be
> A simple locus now, a bell
> The Already There can lay
> Hands on if at any time

It should feel inclined to say
To the lonely—"Here I am,"
To the anxious—"All is well."

Alonzo's address to his son Ferdinand, who will soon be ascending the throne of Milan and perhaps of Naples, is subtle in idea, informal in tone, and solemn in sentiment. Again a somewhat artificial meter, this time of counted syllables, is entirely natural and spontaneous. In the opening stanza the starkly concrete yet somewhat discordant details ("fish see sceptres descending," "broken-down sofa," "mutilated statue") go beyond the realistic to convey a suggestion of the sinister, the foreboding, and the unpredictable, as Alonzo warns his son of the uncertainties even of a royal existence:

Dear Son, when the warm multitudes cry,
Ascend your throne majestically,
But keep in mind the waters where fish
See sceptres descending with no wish
To touch them; sit regal and erect,
But imagine the sands where a crown
Has the status of a broken-down
Sofa or mutilated statue:
Remember as bells and cannon boom
The cold deep that does not envy you,
The sunburnt superficial kingdom
Where a king is an object.

The sea and desert imagery in these lines is developed in every stanza to signify the dreariest ranges of desolation; the sea and the desert are free places, but they are wildernesses and therefore places of alienation from the rest of humanity.[6] Apart from the implications of this imagery, Alonzo's philosophical meaning would not exist. Ferdinand should be warned, Alonzo thinks, that a human being is subject to extreme pressures: the sea and the desert, ice and fire. The sea and the desert—"The sea . . . the symbol of primitive potential power as contrasted with the desert of actualized triviality, of living barbarism versus lifeless decadence" [7]—comprise opposing forces never far from each other nor far from "the temperate city" of man's residence. They are only horrors to

[6] Auden, *The Enchafèd Flood: or, The Romantic Iconography of the Sea* (London, 1951), pp. 25 ff.
[7] *The Enchafèd Flood*, p. 28.

the unreconciled heart which lacks confidence in itself and power to reconcile these discordant entities. By enduring all they may subject us to, "the scorching rocks" and "the bitter treatment of the tide," one may achieve clarity, serenity, wisdom, salvation:

> the whirlwind may arrange your will
> And the deluge release it to find
> The spring in the desert, the fruitful
> Island in the sea, where flesh and mind
> Are delivered from mistrust.

Auden projected the elaborate psychology of the repentant Sebastian through a sestina. In an arresting flash of memory, Sebastian sees himself as he was only a little while before: "To think his death I thought myself alive/ And stalked infected through the blooming day." He now welcomes the negative experiences of failure, exposure, and defeat as positive states which have prevented him from committing a crime. He sees that projected evil in the mind is much more alluring than the actual evil deed: "In dreams all sins are easy, but by day/ It is defeat gives proof we are alive;/ The sword we suffer is the guarded crown." The sestina leaves unsolved to what extent Sebastian's repentance derives from weakness of will or from conscience.

In her villanelle Miranda sees nature, art, and humanity in harmonious unity: "we/ Are linked as children in a circle dancing:/ My Dear One is mine as mirrors are lonely,/ And the high green hill sits always by the sea." On this note of partial reconciliation the speeches by the supporting cast end. The characters have achieved some of the harmony to be found in the completed art work; Miranda's description of the characters "in a circle dancing" is similar to Caliban's description of art as "the excellent order of the dancing ring." In life, of course, an absolute harmony is impossible; witness Antonio's rejection of the virginal Miranda's spirituality in his comments which follow her villanelle. The "restored relation" between the human and the divine—celebrated in Caliban's concluding words—has at least been adumbrated through Prospero's aesthetic magic. Antonio's consistent menace may ultimately make the "restored relation" more genuine by his very threat to it.

"The Sea and the Mirror" is a philosophically unified and skillfully constructed work of art, much more carefully wrought than "For the Time Being" and "The Age of Anxiety," in which Auden was too explicitly Christian perhaps for the requirements of his art to be uppermost in his mind. The transcendental subjectivism and the Christian values, expressed or implied in the poetry of this period, form the complex, however, out of which Auden was to write during the late 1940's and 1950's. If none of his volumes is individually as significant as *On This Island* or *Another Time,* still when we consider as an entity *Nones* (1950), *The Shield of Achilles* (1956), and *Homage to Clio* (1960), we are impressed by the continuing vitality and relevance of Auden's poetry. The bulk of first-rate work during the last fifteen years is less than in the period 1930-45, but there are a number of poems written in late years which may achieve a classic status: "In Praise of Limestone," "Prime," "Nones," "The Fall of Rome," "The Chimeras," "A Walk After Dark," and "A Duet" from *Nones;* "The Shield of Achilles," "Fleet Visit," "The Proof," and "Nocturne I" from *The Shield of Achilles;* and "Reflections in a Forest," "First Things First," "Sabbath," "Friday's Child," and "Secondary Epic" from *Homage to Clio.*

If Auden's poetry of the last fifteen years were to be compressed into a single volume, the solidity rather than the slenderness of the accomplishment would be more apparent. In writing on Bernard Shaw, Auden once stated that a writer is great when he transcends both simple acceptance and revolt;[8] this has been, I feel, the source of Auden's own enduring interest since the early 1940's for most readers. If from some points of view, Auden's recent work represents a falling off from the exuberant fertility of the late 1930's, from another point of view we witness a deliberate reaching out to extend the provinces of poetry.

The keeping alive of the poetic impulse may have been the result of a transplantation to a new environment in the early 1940's. In America Auden renewed the powers which had been exhausted in the England of the 1930's; in becoming, as it were, a citizen of the world, his vision was widened and made more firm. America exposed him more closely to the leveling processes of a technological civilization and forced him to come to terms more quickly with violent pressures from without. To Auden's stay in America we owe some of the poems in *Another Time,* the long poems of the 1940's, and some excellent poetry composed more recently. As he felt his isolation intensify in an alien environment, his need for philosophic and spiritual assurance increased, and he turned to existentialist thinkers and the work of Reinhold Niebuhr for guidance during this time of crisis. Possibly as an American citizen, since 1956 residing part of the year in England, Auden may again achieve some of

[8] "The Fabian Figaro," in Louis Kronenberger, ed., *George Bernard Shaw: A Critical Survey* (New York, 1953), p. 153. This essay was written in 1942.

the radical reorientation of his views which the move to America once gave him. He may yet give us another poem of the freshness and vigor of "The Sea and the Mirror"; and he once again may exemplify to the full his own definition of the great poet as simultaneously a realist, romanticist, and ironist.[9]

[9] Howard Griffin, "Conversation on Cornelia Street: A Dialogue with W. H. Auden," *Poetry,* LXXXIII (November, 1953), 97.

Auden's *New Year Letter:* A New Style of Architecture

by Edward Callan

W. H. Auden has often suggested that one function of the artist, in every age, is to discover new forms to express the unique insights of his time. For example, Auden dwells on the kinship between neo-classical style and the ideas of an age that admired reason and order, and he points to the changes in style that accompanied the self-conscious pre-occupation of the artist of the Age of Romanticism. In particular, Auden draws attention to a significant change in the form of tragedy following the emergence of the Christian conception of the nature of man. While the Greek tragic character, for example, Oedipus, *suffers* his allotted fate, the tragic character in the drama of Christendom, for example, Macbeth, *becomes* his later self through his own moral choices. Auden points out that in *Oedipus Rex,* since only the hero's situation, and not his character, changes: "unity of time is not only possible but right and proper"; and he suggests that if Shakespeare had handled the story of Oedipus, the tragic hero would confront successive choices of action demanding "not only a different plot, but also a different formal structure and a different poetic style." In brief, Auden holds that a change, or a shift in emphasis, in the answers to man's fundamental questions about his situation "changes the style and subject-matter of poetry and the poet's conception of his function." Auden's penchant for experimenting with form may suggest prolonged interest in this theory; and an early sonnet, "Sir, no man's enemy," surely epitomizes it in the concluding petition: "look shining at/ New styles of architecture, a change of heart."

Critics generally concede that Auden's work following his emigration to America in 1939 is grounded in a Christian outlook transcending his earlier preference for near-Marxist social theory and his earlier concept

"Auden's *New Year Letter:* A New Style of Architecture" by Edward Callan. From *Renascence: A Critical Journal of Letters,* XVI (1963), 13-19.

of personality derived from Freud, Groddeck, and Homer Lane. In their varying estimates of Auden's later work, commentators have tended to stress the "change of heart" and to ignore the architecture.

In seeking an appropriate architecture for modern themes Auden found useful models in Jung's theories on the psyche, and Kierkegaard's all-embracing notional scheme of categories. These conceptual schemes provided original structural devices for Auden's four later major works: *New Year Letter; The Sea and the Mirror; For the Time Being;* and *The Age of Anxiety;* as well as new sources of metaphor for many of his later lyrics.

Auden's first long poem of the 1940's, *New Year Letter,* is an initial experiment in an architectural method which he later refined and developed in the other long works. *New York Letter* is a simple construction: it is a three-part poem in which the parts correspond to Kierkegaard's triad of Aesthetic, Ethical, and Religious spheres. The subject-matter of the poem is the problem of order in each of these spheres and therefore might be said to resemble Dante's *Divine Comedy* in its structure as well as in its theme which ultimately transcends local and temporal order and includes the restoration of Divine order.

Kierkegaard's triad may categorize either individual persons or particular periods of history. The Aesthetic person may, like the artist, see things as beautiful or ugly, or, like the gambler, see them as governed by chance, or even by magic. The Ethical person—the philosopher or logician—envisions a world governed by rational laws, and describes man's actions as right or wrong, not as beautiful or ugly. The Religious person is one whose faith transcends the limitations of fate or reason and accepts what, to the Ethical mind, is absurd, and, to the Aesthetic mind, incomprehensible. Furthermore, the categories permit such classification of historical periods as this: the period influenced by the Aesthetic religion of the Greek pantheon, the period that discovered the Ethical "good" of philosophy, and the period of "revealed religion in which neither is destroyed or ignored, but the Aesthetic is dethroned and the Ethical fulfilled."

The three parts of *New Year Letter* correspond in both structure and subject-matter with Kierkegaard's three categories. Part I corresponds to the sphere of the Aesthetic; its subject is the relation of art and the artistic vocation to ultimate order; its subdivisions resemble a series of figurative devices or devices of art; and it culminates in a key metaphor drawn from the Greek religion. Part II corresponds to the sphere of the Ethical; its subject is the variety of intellectual systems—dualisms or monisms—that logicians have proposed as ultimate order; the verse is rhetorical rather than figurative; and it culminates in a key metaphor concerning the "double-focus" of dialectical logic. Part III corresponds to the spheres of the Aesthetic and Ethical reconciled; its subject is Love "set in order," or restored through penitence; its literary method is a purgatorial Quest analogous to Dante's *Divine Comedy,* developed through an orchestral arrangement of such themes as Being and Becoming, Time and Space, and the One and the Many; and it culminates in a hymn to the Holy Trinity.

A few representative passages may illustrate more fully these correspondences. Excluding the introductory and concluding paragraphs, which fulfill their necessary functions, the separate verse-paragraphs in the body of Part I seem intended to approximate to six artistic devices in the following order: extended metaphor, personification, paradox, apostrophe, dramatization and analogy. Auden thus embellishes the part of *New Year Letter* corresponding to the Aesthetic sphere with an appropriate galaxy of art forms. Each of the figurative devices reflects some aspect of the order possible to art. The apostrophe, for example, is addressed to those "great masters who have shown mankind/ An order it has yet to find," and who, despite the conflicting demands of their art and their lives, have created lasting examples of artistic order. The final analogy, on the other hand, laments the inability of art to erase the guilt of social disorder. This theme is presented in the form of an analogy to the detective story in which the interest, as Auden has said elsewhere, is the "dialectic of innocence and guilt." So, here, in "Our parish of immediacy," all are suspects and involved/ Until the mystery is solved." A brief and witty comparison between police methods in democracies and in dictatorships extends the scene of the crime from "Our parish of immediacy" to the global conflicts in which the guilt for national and international crimes involves all mankind. The concluding paragraph laments the helplessness of poetry to rescue the social order, but finds some hope in the ambivalent *form* of the *Aesthetic* pronouncements of the Delphic Oracle: "For through the Janus of a joke/ The candid psychopompos spoke." [ll.305-307]

Having dealt with the limitations and possibilities of art and the Aesthetic mode for the restoration of order, Auden turns in Part II to the limitations and possibilities of the intellect and of those systems, ideologies and Utopias which human reason has, from time to time, proposed as ultimate order. This is the sphere of the Ethical: the region of moral choice. It is also the sphere of philosophy and of logic, rhetoric, and argument. Since Part II is concerned with the exposition of ideas rather than with figurative representation, Auden attempts a different kind of poetic expression. Even a cursory examination of Part II shows noticeable difference in the texture of the verse. Except, again, for the introductory and concluding paragraphs which are highly figurative, the devices of art and extended metaphor characteristic of Part I are replaced in the body of Part II by figures of rhetoric, such as antithesis, paradox, and chiasmal construction—common vehicles of Augustan wit.

This section is composed of a series of arguments about the defects of two kinds of intellectual scheme for universal order: dualism, which is the denial of any relation between the universal and the particular, and monism, the assumption that the laws peculiar to one realm are the universal laws from which all others are derived. The main antagonist in the dialectic of good and evil is Mephistopheles: "But who, though, is the Prince of Lies/ If not the Spirit-that-denies." Throughout Part II, Mephistopheles is adept at using dialectics in the manner of the skeptic in order to make the opposite of any conclusion equally probable. The transition from the arguments on the errors of dualism to those on monism is made in a long verse-paragraph which reveals the devil to be both dualist and monist, i.e., the source of both the evils against unity. He is "the great schismatic who/ First split creation into two"; yet he is pledged to a single course, "to Rule-by-Sin":

> And his neurotic longing mocks
> Him with its self-made paradox
> To be both god and dualist.
>
> [ll.571-572]

The concluding paragraph of Part II seizes upon the double approach of the devil to introduce the key image of this section of the poem: "So, hidden in his hocus-pocus/ There lies the gift of double focus." That is to say, the devil's cynical double-talk, ironically, resembles a dialectic, such as Kierkegaard's, which aims at the reconciliation of opposites:

> So hidden in his hocus-pocus,
> There lies the gift of double focus,
> That magic lamp which looks so dull
> And utterly impractical
> Yet, if Aladdin use it right,
> Can be the sesame to the light.
>
> [ll.827-832]

This image of the double focus of dialectic climaxes the Ethical theme of Part II as the ambivalent Janus symbol climaxes the Aesthetic theme of Part I.

Both of these parts, which together constitute slightly less than half of the poem, may be looked upon as parallel prologues to Part III which broaches the idea of the reconciliation of the Aesthetic and Ethical modes on a higher plane—the Religious, in Kierkegaard's scheme—or in Auden's words: "the restoration of the state of grace in which the aesthetic and the ethical are as one." Auden often comments on the impossibility of representing this mode through the medium of art, but in his essay "Preface to Kierkegaard" he remarks with regard to the religious significance of temporal acts: "The one artistic medium that can represent such things is music, but only as a paradox, only because music does not represent or imitate anything, but is itself the exact opposite of the religious, pure, sensual immediacy." Whether or not Auden had such a relationship in mind when composing Part III of *New Year Letter,* its structure, with its recurrent themes and contrapuntal arrangements, is analogous to symphonic orchestration.

The theme of the Quest dominates the opening of the section where the penitential way is presented as the only alternative to presumption or denial for creatures endowed with free-will. From this theme arises in turn the theme of the individual threatened with anonymity in modern mechanized societies. Then the image of the two Atlases, "the one / The public space where acts are done" and the other, "the inner space/ Of private ownership," prepares the way for the theme of the inner consciousness of the individual and also for the theme of human societies widely separated in time and space. The final stages of Part III return to the theme of the solitary quest as the only solution to man's plight. As Part III draws to a close, with the theme of time still in the mechanized age, the space theme moves to awakening Asia: "Clocks shoo the childhood from its face." Looking forward in time to Asia's future, the nineteenth paragraph envisions "what ought to be/ The nature of society":

> How readily would we become
> The seamless live continuum
> Of supple and coherent stuff,
> Whose form is truth, whose content love. . . .
> [ll.1589-1592]

The penultimate paragraph of Part III takes the form of an invocation to the Holy Trinity. Here, through masterly use of assonance and internal rhyme, Auden succeeds in imposing a devotional tone on the octosyllables of *New Year Letter* which, although artfully varied, have much of the sparkle of Hudibrastics up to this point—in keeping, no doubt, with the poem's "reverent frivolity." The invocation opens with the lines:

> O Unicorn among the cedars,
> To whom no magic charm can lead us,
> White childhood moving like a sigh,
> Through the green woods unharmed in thy
> Sophisticated innocence,
> To call thy true love to the dance. . . .
> [ll.1651-1656]

These opening lines may illustrate how Auden consistently draws upon Kierkegaard's categories for the imagery of the concluding hymn. For example, since magic is encompassed by the Aesthetic sphere, the line, "To whom no magic charm can lead us" is a re-affirmation of the view that art cannot directly represent the Religious sphere. But if art cannot represent the Religious sphere directly, it *can* provide analogies for its perfect order. One common analogy for both the perfect order of art and the ultimate order of paradise is the dance; and to express this, Auden borrows (with altered pronoun) the line, "To call my true love to the dance," from a medieval lyric in which the speaker is Christ.

This final invocation to the Holy Trinity furnishes a device to climax the Religious theme of Part III comparable to the dialectical trick by which the devil's "hocus-pocus" became the "gift of double focus" to climax the Ethical theme of Part II, and comparable also to the Janus symbol for the ambivalence of art which climaxes the Aesthetic theme of Part I. It seems clear, then, that Auden solved the problem of form for the philosophical themes of *New Year Letter* by constructing a framework resembling a formal analogue for the poem's subject-matter: that is to say, the framework reflects the subject-matter almost as a Chinese ideograph reflects the idea it represents.

The problem of finding a satisfactory vehicle for long works has perplexed modern poets, and few have solved it satisfactorily. The style of the major works of, for example, Milton or Spenser has little attraction for modern imitators; for the allegorical habit of mind is no longer living, and the novelist has appropriated the epic framework and the narrative method. Lacking a self-consistent cosmology—such as Dante's—to support a complex symbolic structure, some moderns like Blake and Yeats have constructed private symbolic systems. Others have experimented in a variety of ways: T. S. Eliot, for example, successfully developed long works by patterning his themes in a manner analogous to musical composition, but there is little general agreement on the degree of success attending most modern attempts at works of magnitude, as in the cases, for example, of Hart Crane's *The Bridge* or Ezra Pound's *Cantos.*

The choice of Kierkegaard's scheme of categories as unifying principle for a major poetic composition served Auden in two ways; for this choice provided the necessary bounds for an imaginative construction and at the same time, paradoxically, allowed the imagination free play over "all that is," since Kierkegaard's triad is not a restrictive, but an all-embracing, notional scheme. The poet is not chained by a set philosophic formulae, because the essence of Kierkegaard's thought opposes both formula and system. His own thought is not set forth in systematic treatises but in such literary forms as the journal, the diary, the symposium or the character sketch, which keep the existent individual always in view. Auden's choice of a personal letter as the *genre* of *New Year Letter* is therefore consistent with the whole scheme of the poem. Those who have viewed the poem as a "loosely constructed dissertation" are at least half right, but they miss Auden's insistence throughout the poem on reconciling dialectical opposites. The poem attempts to represent the dialectical relationship of Freedom and Necessity in its structure as well as in its matter, so that the question of the formality or informality of its structure is not resolved by an "either/or" but is encompassed by a "both/and." It is, in the words already quoted, both "supple and coherent stuff," or, like James Joyce's puns, both trivial and quadrivial.

Ideally, Kierkegaard's philosophy cannot be formulated; it can only be acted out, and the literary form best suited to representing it is the drama. Auden's later major works, while continuing to depend on the scheme of categories for a unifying principle, are cast in dramatic forms which permit, for example, in *For the Time Being,* the representation of Herod as the type of the rational or Ethical man, and of St. Joseph as the type of "the Religious hero" who, like Abraham, must transcend the Ethical sphere and accept the "absurd" on the basis of faith alone.

I have suggested that Auden refined and developed, in other major works, this new style of architecture in which the structure of the work is a formal analogue for its subject-matter. *The Sea and the Mirror: A Commentary on Shakespeare's "The Tempest"* provides an interesting example of this. The theme of *The Sea and the Mirror* is the relationship between art and reality. The structure of this poem is comparable to a triptych: the first panel represents the artist; the second, the work of art; and the third, the audience. In Part I, Prospero, the "personified type of the creative," becomes aware of death as a reality he cannot conjure with. His farewell to Ariel is developed in three stages analogous to Kierkegaard's triad. Part II is an elaborate pageant corresponding to Prospero's masque in *The Tempest*. The group of characters from Ferdinand to Miranda who are "linked as children in a circle dancing" represent the ideal order possible in art; and the arrangement also suggests a "Utopian" social order as Alonso holds the center and the courtly and rustic characters are proportioned on either side of him between the lovers. The attitude of Antonio who stands withdrawn from the group represents the tension between his Ethical world of "will" and their Aesthetic world of "wish"—a tension present in all Christian art. Part III, "Caliban to the Audience," is an artful symposium in which Caliban echoes the Ethical and Aesthetic attitudes of the audience to the relationship of art and reality.

In *For the Time Being* the unifying principle of structure rests on a fusion of the traditional elements of the Nativity play with Kierkegaard's triad, and in a somewhat similar manner the architectural framework of *The Age of Anxiety* rests on a fusion of Kierkegaard's scheme with Jung's "maps" of the psyche. Auden's continued use of this method would argue his satisfaction with the initial experiment in *New Year Letter.*

Auden had changed the style and the subject-matter of his poetry to accord with the shift in emphasis in his own questions about man's situation. Had he also changed his conception of the poet's function? The tone of *New Year Letter* shows that Kierkegaard's dialectical method helped Auden to solve this problem too. Some have felt that the conflict between Montaigne's "doubt" and Kierkegaard's "faith" throughout *New Year Letter* indicates Auden's unsure stance; but could this not be merely a presentation of the dialectical tension between the Ethical and Religious spheres? However this may be, *New Year Letter* certainly resolves the conflict between "preacher" and "poet" that some have found in Auden; for this poem is, like *Macbeth,* a product of the art of Christendom which must reconcile the Ethical and the Aesthetic and present "serious" subject-matter through the "frivolous" medium of art. Hence the deliberate serio-comic tone of a poem embracing spheres inimical to the purely Aesthetic: "For through the Janus of a joke/ The candid psychopompos spoke."

For the Time Being

by Monroe K. Spears

Auden's mother, who was devout and to whom he had been very close,[1] died in 1941. *For the Time Being,* dedicated to her memory, was written in 1941-2.[2] The subtitle is "A Christmas Oratorio"; it is of course too long to be set in its entirety, but an abridgement of it was set by the American composer, Melvin Levy, and performed in New York a few years ago. It follows the oratorio form faithfully, except that musical setting is not essential: i.e. it is an oratorio to be spoken or read. In many respects, the oratorio form enables Auden to achieve effects he sought in the plays: there is no dramatic illusion, no identification, and no dramatic characterization. There is, so to speak, a built-in alienation effect, since in the oratorio singers use only their voices to represent their roles, without acting, and the audience is aware continuously of the singers as singers as well as participants in the drama; hence the characters move in two dimensions, as, simultaneously, the unique historical characters and the moderns who are representing them. The oratorio differs from the plays in presenting a story both historical and thoroughly familiar, so that the traditional Christmas pageant or tableau can be

[1] *Letters from Iceland,* p. 239: "The Church of Saint Aidan at Smallheath to my mother/Where she may pray for this poor world and me"; p. 204, "We imitate our loves: well, neighbours say/I grow more like my mother every day." In "A Literary Transference" (1940) Auden says that Hardy "looked like my father: that broad unpampered moustache, bald forehead and deeply lined sympathetic face belonged to the other world of feeling and sensation (for I, like my mother, was a thinking-intuitive)."

[2] It was "begun in Ann Arbor and finished before I came to Swarthmore" (letter to M.K.S., March 21, 1962). Several portions were published in periodicals: "At the Manger" in *Commonweal,* Dec. 25, 1942; "Herod Considers the Massacre of the Innocents" in *Harper's,* Dec. 1943; "After Christmas" (the Narrator's final speech) in *Harper's.* Jan. 1944.

suggested, as well as the miracle play, and the lighter elements of popular song and contemporary language can more effectively surprise the reader who expects a wholly solemn, elevated work. The verse is an equivalent for the kind of distancing produced by musical setting, and in variety of forms and meters it succeeds in producing many of the effects of music. The chorus expresses collective feelings and attitudes in a formal, often exalted manner, while the narrator, voluble, articulate, and thoroughly modern, expresses the other side of the contemporary consciousness. Together, they mediate between the audience and the action more effectively than any of Auden's previous choruses or announcers.

From the religious point of view, the form of the Christmas oratorio immediately suggests three kinds of meaning: (1) the unique Incarnation; (2) by association with Christmas and with other Christmas oratorios, plays, pageants, and the like, the annual attempt in Christendom to apprehend and experience the event as the center of the Christian year; (3) the constant attempt of Christians to understand, make viable, and in some sense repeat the Incarnation in their daily lives. *For the Time Being* generally succeeds in keeping the reader simultaneously aware of all three of these meanings. The piece is the fullest and most balanced expression of Auden's religious attitudes; the ideas and dominant images that have been seen partially and transitionally in other poems here may be seen in their final place as part of an ordered whole. Much could be said of the religious background of the piece (the respective influences of Kierkegaard, Niebuhr, Williams, Cochrane, and Eliot) and of the relation of the ideas in it to those Auden had been expounding both in prose and verse; but I shall forego this kind of discussion in favor of what will, I hope, be more immediately useful—an interpretative commentary keeping close to the work itself.

The first section, "Advent," represents in the historical sense the exhaustion and despair of the ancient world on the eve of Christ's birth. (As we have seen, Auden had been much concerned in his prose writings with defining the philosophical impasse of the classical world and the parallel with the present.) But two other levels are constantly present: the perennial situation of man without Christ, and, as the title indicates, the annual Church season of preparation for Christmas—the Incarnation, that is, is presented as a recurring as well as a unique event. The opening chorus is trimeter, iambic but with one anapaest to the line; it is probably modeled (as earlier critics have suggested) on the final chorus of Dryden's "Secular Masque," but has a very different effect. suggesting plodding weariness and monotony. The semi-chorus interrupts twice, in very irregular trimeter, to describe the loss of hope of a secular savior; great Hercules is not only unable to reinvigorate the empire but is, himself, utterly lost. The chorus plods on in the original meter: "Darkness and snow descend," and "The evil and armed draw near." Into their lamentations breaks the rational, mundane voice of the narrator. He complains that an outrageous novelty has been introduced, so that "nothing/ We learnt before It was there is now of the slightest use"; as if the room had "changed places/ With the room behind the mirror over the fireplace." What has happened, he says, is that the locus of reality has shifted: "the world of space where events re-occur is still there,/ Only now it's no longer real; the real one is nowhere/ Where time never moves and nothing can ever happen." (This central theme of the relation of Time to Reality, of the entry of the Eternal into the world of Time as the center of history, and of the resentment and resistance with which the "outrageous novelty" is greeted by human beings is inevitably rendered sometimes in tones and images recalling its great modern master, Eliot.) In this first speech the narrator continues to explain the consequences to man's sense of identity and relation to the self: "although there's a person we know all about/ Still bearing our name and loving himself as before,/ That person has become a fiction. . . ." The chorus chants in despair, "Alone, alone, about a dreadful wood/ Of conscious evil runs a lost mankind" [3] and concludes, "We who must die demand a miracle," since "Nothing can save us that is possible." The section ends with a recitative and chorus; the former explores the paradoxical nature of religious truth in long, six-stress lines that are precise and restrained in diction ("The Real is what will strike you as really absurd") and introducing the garden and desert symbols ("For the garden is the only place there is, but you will not find it/ Until you have looked for it everywhere and found nowhere that is not a desert"); the Chorus, written in elegiacs (alternating dactylic hexameter and pentameter) and elevated in diction, and hence reminiscent of Greek poetry, describes man's condition and his peculiar temptations and difficulties as compared to the other creatures.

> Alas, his genius is wholly for envy; alas,
> The vegetative sadness of lakes, the locomotive beauty
> Of choleric beasts of prey, are nearer than he
> To the dreams that deprive him of sleep, the powers that compel him to idle
> To his amorous nymphs and his sanguine athletic gods.

[3] There is an obvious allusion to the beginning of the *Divine Comedy*.

How can his knowledge protect his desire for truth from illusion?
How can he wait without idols to worship. . . .

The second section, "The Annunciation," begins with the four faculties—intuition, feeling, sensation, thought—that were once one but were dissociated by the Fall. They identify themselves in the manner of abstractions (e.g. the Seven Deadly Sins) in medieval drama, and the dimeter quatrain they employ at first recalls Goethe's *Faust;* their second speeches are in dramatic blank verse. They are the "Ambiguous causes/ Of all temptation" and "lure men either/ To death or salvation"; their function here is to report what happens in the Garden. The Annunciation proper is expressed in a series of beautiful metaphysical lyrics, majestic and complex for Gabriel and exalted and intense for Mary. Gabriel makes explicit the parallel with Eve in her earlier Garden: she, "in love with her own will/ Denied the will of Love and fell"; but "What her negation wounded, may/ Your affirmation heal today":

Love's will requires your own, that in
The flesh whose love you do not know,
Love's knowledge into flesh may grow.

Mary rejoices that God, as a pledge of his love for the world, "Should ask to wear me,/ From now to their wedding day,/ For an engagement ring." The conceit is brilliant and precise, but the tone of the last image seems to me incongruous and anticlimactic. This fault, if real, is no more than the result of the risk inherent in this metaphysical style. More unfortunate is the refrain in the final part of the section, in which the chorus rejoices because *"There's a Way. There's a Voice."* For American readers at least, this suggests both the Glory Road of the revivalist and the American, or democratic, Way of Life of the propagandist. Auden may have been misled by the musical analogy here. As a sung choral refrain, the line would probably be unobjectionable, but italicized on the page, it stands out, and the contractions with their suggestion of informality are incongruous with the capitalized abstractions.

The third section, "The Temptation of St. Joseph," begins audaciously in the vein of the music hall or popular song. Joseph is made very much the average man trying to have faith in spite of appearances; he asks for one reason for believing in divine justice, "one/ Important and elegant proof/ That what my Love had done/ Was really at your will/ And that your will is Love." But Gabriel answers only, "No, you must believe;/ Be silent, and sit still" [4]—thus defining the nature of faith. The narrator comments amusingly on the relations between the sexes, concluding by observing that Joseph and Mary must be man and wife as if nothing had occurred; for faith abolishes the distinction between the usual and the exceptional: "To choose what is difficult all one's days/ As if it were easy, that is faith. Joseph, praise." The section closes with a brilliant semi-chorus in which Joseph and Mary are invoked to pray for various types of sinners: first, the romantic lovers "Misled by moonlight and the rose" who hope to regain innocence through knowledge of the flesh, believe "Simultaneous passions make/ One eternal chastity"; then the "independent embryos" (i.e., presumably, children in the womb) who exhibit the original sin in "every definite decision/ To improve"—even in the "germ-cell's primary division"; finally, the bourgeoisie, the "proper and conventional," with their "indolent fidelity" and their habit-forming "Domestic hatred," their willed disease. Auden still describes this type with special acerbity:

> O pray for our salvation
> Who take the prudent way,
> Believing we shall be exempted
> From the general condemnation
> Because our self-respect is tempted
> To incest not adultery. . . .

Finally as types of the "common ungifted" human being and of marriage, Joseph and Mary are invoked to "Redeem for the dull the/ Average Way."

Section four, "The Summons," forms the dramatic climax, in which mere human wisdom is contrasted with the Christian revelation. Historically, the Magi reveal the inadequacy of classical speculative philosophy, while the Fugal-Chorus in ironic praise of Caesar reveals the inadequacy of ancient statecraft or political philosophy; but the parallel between the years one and 1941 is explicit, and the terms more modern than ancient. In this section Auden has the special problem of avoiding both the powerful influence of Eliot's "Journey of the Magi" and the clichés of Christmas pageants. He manages this by divesting the Magi of their customary solemn impressiveness and transferring it to the Star, which begins by pronouncing the "doom of orthodox sophrosyne," of

[4] Cf. Psalm 46:10 and the "Prayer for Quiet Confidence" in the *Book of Common Prayer*.

the classical wisdom of moderation; the faith which replaces it offers no security, but is like the fairy-tale "Glassy Mountain where are no/ Footholds for logic" or a "Bridge of Dread/ Where knowledge but increases vertigo." [5] The Wise Men speak in stanzas characterized by internal rhyme and a rollicking anapaestic beat, but breaking down into formless prose in the latter part of the stanza to represent frustration and confusion. The first one is a natural scientist: "With rack and screw I put Nature through/ A thorough inquisition"; but her reaction to the investigator (or torturer) made her unreliable; so he follows the Star "to discover how to be truthful now." The second Wise Man has put his faith in the constant flow of Time, but has discovered that the Present disappears under analysis: "With envy, terror, rage, regret,/ We anticipate or remember but never are." He follows the star "to discover how to be living *now*" (my italics). The third has been a kind of social scientist, hoping to make passion philanthropic by introducing the concept "Ought";[6] but calculating the greatest good for the greatest number "left no time for affection," and he follows the star "to discover how to be loving now." The three of them together sing that after their journey "At least we know for certain that we are three old sinners" and together they seek "To discover how to be human now." The star tells them they must endure terror and tribulation, but if they keep faith all will be well.

In strong contrast comes the voice of the secular state, Caesar's proclamation, followed by a Fugal-Chorus in ironic praise of him. The state is more our own than that of Augustus, and the Seven Kingdoms Caesar has conquered are the boasted achievements of our civilization: Abstract Idea includes everything from language to philosophy, and is the basis of the rest; Natural Cause is obviously the natural sciences (considered as a substitute religion); Infinite Number is mathematics; Credit Exchange is the monetary system and finance capitalism; Inorganic Giants are clearly machines; Organic Dwarfs seem to be drugs, which can not only control disease, pain, and worry but stimulate emotions; the last, Popular Soul, is of course propaganda and the techniques of mass psy-

[5] Cf. Auden's volume of selections from Kierkegaard, p. 30: "Christianity is certainly not melancholy, it is, on the contrary, glad tidings—for the melancholy; to the frivolous it is certainly not glad tidings, for it wishes first of all to make them serious. That is the road we all have to take—over the Bridge of Sighs into eternity."

[6] The image is a brilliant one that perhaps needs paraphrase: observing that the Venus of the Soma (i.e., the biological Eros) is myopic, he hopes that his moral imperative will rectify the optical errors (lens-flare and lens-coma) that mislead the sensual eye.

chology. In style, the repetition of formulas and patterns does produce a fugal effect, and the musical analogy is amusing. This is followed by the narrator's news broadcast, fusing modern and ancient, and concluding once more with the secular boast, "Our great Empire shall be secure for a thousand years." But this is followed immediately by the confession that "no one is taken in, at least not all of the time":

> In our bath, or the subway, or the middle of the night,
> We know very well we are not unlucky but evil,
> That the dream of a Perfect State or No State at all,
> To which we fly for refuge, is a part of our punishment.

And he points out, in orthodox fashion, that societies and epochs are transient details, important only as transmitting "an everlasting opportunity/ That the Kingdom of Heaven may come, not in our present/ And not in our future, but in the Fullness of Time." The section ends with a prayer in chorale form, recalling in meter and diction the traditional hymn (and providing an interesting contrast with the parody hymn "Not, Father, further . . ." in *The Orators*).

"The Vision of the Shepherds," the next section, interprets the shepherds in traditional fashion as the poor, though they are modern massmen rather than pastoral types: they keep the mechanism going. This section alone would be enough to confute those who say Auden lacks understanding of or sympathy with the common man; it is shrewd, amusing, and without condescension. The shepherds observe that those who sentimentalize poverty and ignorance have "done pretty well for themselves," while those who insist that the poor are important and should stand up for their rights also insist that the individual doesn't matter. But, they say, what is real about us all "is that each of us is waiting" for the Good News. The Chorus of Angels then announces to them the "ingression of Love" and the consequent Gospel: the old "Authoritarian/ Constraint is replaced/ By the Covenant,/ And a city based/ On love and consent/ Suggested to men. . . ." The chorus adds that "after today/ The children of men/ May be certain that/ The Father Abyss/ Is affectionate/ To all Its creatures,/ All, all, all of them. . . ."

"At the Manger" presents the traditional tableau with Wise Men and Shepherds. Mary sings a tender lullaby in modified sapphics (five instead of three eleven-syllable lines, followed by a short line of four instead of the customary five syllables), reflecting that her human flesh and maternal care can only bring the Child anxiety, tears, sorrow, and death. The

Wise Men and Shepherds characterize their former selves contrastingly, the death-wish ("arrogant longing to attain the tomb") versus regression ("sullen wish to go back to the womb"), "Exceptional conceit" with "average fear," as they bring, instead of the traditional gifts, their bodies and minds to the Child. The Wise Men have discovered that "Love is more serious than Philosophy/ Who sees no humour in her observation/ That Truth is knowing that we know we lie." Repeating (in a virtuosic display) the same rhymes eight times, they explain why human identity and personality is valuable: "Love's possibilities of realisation/ Require an Otherness that can say *I*" and what the true reality of space and time is: "Space is the Whom our loves are needed by,/ Time is our choice of How to love and Why."

"The Meditation of Simeon," in contrast to the stress on Love in the preceding section, emphasizes the philosophical meaning of the Incarnation. Since Simeon is the type of the convert, this is appropriate. As has often been observed, it is probably the best brief exposition of Auden's religious position, or at least of its intellectual aspect. It is in prose—the first time prose has been used in the oratorio—interspersed with one-line alliterative comments by the chorus, which render emotionally what Simeon has been saying in prose. Simeon's style is eloquent, without any particular mask or characterization; his language is that of the modern intellectual. (There is no resemblance whatever to Eliot's "Song for Simeon.") He explains first that before the Incarnation could take place, it was necessary that the nature and effects of the Fall become clear, that man understand his original sin and the failure of remedy or escape: "The Word could not be made Flesh until men had reached a state of absolute contradiction between clarity and despair in which they would have no choice but either to accept absolutely or to reject absolutely. . . ." But now "that which hitherto we could only passively fear as the incomprehensible I AM, henceforth we may actively love with comprehension that THOU ART." Simeon then proceeds to spell out the intellectual consequences. First, since "He is in no sense a symbol," this existence gives value to all others. The distinction between sin and temptation is clarified, "for in Him we become fully conscious of Necessity as our freedom to be tempted, and of Freedom as our necessity to have faith." The meaning of Time is illuminated, for "the course of History is predictable in the degree to which all men love themselves, and spontaneous in the degree to which each man loves God and through Him his neighbour." (This passage has been cited earlier in the discussion of Love in the shorter poems of this period, as has the one about the elimination of the distinction between the Average and the Exceptional, the Common Man and the Hero: "disaster is not the impact of a curse upon a few great families, but issues continually from the hubris of every tainted will. Every invalid is Roland . . . , every stenographer Brunnhilde. . . .") A further aesthetic consequence is that the Ridiculous is no longer confined to the Ugly; since "of themselves all men are without merit, all are ironically assisted to their comic bewilderment by the Grace of God"; hence the logic of fairy tales represents spiritual truth: "Every Cabinet Minister is the woodcutter's simple-minded son to whom the fishes and the crows are always whispering the whereabouts of the Dancing Water. . . ." Similarly, every situation is now essentially as interesting as any other: "Every tea-table is a battlefield littered with old catastrophes . . . every martyrdom an occasion for flip cracks and sententious oratory." Finally, Simeon explains the metaphysical value of the Trinity: since the Word is united to the Flesh, the One and the Many are simultaneously revealed as real, so that neither can be denied. Truth is One, but "the possibilities of real knowledge are as many as are the creatures in the very real and most exciting universe that God creates with and for His love. . . ." Simeon concludes by praying that "we may depart from our anxiety into His peace."

As Simeon is the type of the Christian convert and intellectual, Herod, in the next section, "The Massacre of the Innocents," is the type of the liberal intellectual, the Manager and Apollonian we have seen in the shorter poems, dedicated to service, progress, and the advancement of reason, now confronted with the Irrational. His speech, which counterbalances Simeon's as the only other one in prose, is a deft fusion of ancient and modern: Herod is both the historical character and the liberal of the late 1930s, trying to cope with the threats of war and fascism.[7] His speech is witty, amusing, and highly persuasive on its own premises: his long struggle to establish law and order and push back superstition is doomed by this irruption of the Irrational. In terms sometimes recalling Yeats's play, "The Resurrection," and sometimes recalling Nietzsche, he gloomily predicts the consequences—Reason will be replaced by Revelation, Idealism by Materialism, Justice by Pity. "Naturally this

[7] Randall Jarrell, in his brilliant but inimical essay, "Freud to Paul: The Stages of Auden's Ideology," *Partisan Review,* Fall 1945, complains that Auden chose Herod rather than Pilate to represent the typical Liberal: "We are so *used* to rejecting Herod as a particularly bogey-ish Churchill that Auden can count on our going right on rejecting him when he is presented as Sir Stafford Cripps" (p. 442). One wonders whether Jarrell can actually have thought Auden was free to replace Herod by Pilate, as if they were both fictional characters.

cannot be allowed to happen," and he concludes reluctantly that he must send for the military to prevent it. Petulantly, he complains, "Why can't people be sensible? I don't want to be horrid. Why can't they see that the notion of a finite God is absurd?" It is unreasonable that a decision as to the existence of God should be up to Herod: "How dare He allow me to decide?" (In other words, he refuses to go beyond the secular and rejects the existentialist Choice.) He concludes uneasily and self-pityingly, "I've tried to be good. I brush my teeth every night. I haven't had sex for a month. I object. I'm a liberal. I want everyone to be happy. I wish I had never been born."

The Soldiers speak next, their callous brutality and cynical humor embodying the perennial cruelty and evil of human nature; their speech comes after Herod's with massive irony, reminding us that the end in practice of Herod's plausible speech has been the decision to massacre the Innocents. The fantasy and exaggeration of the Soldiers' speech and its ironic tall-story "good fellowship" prevents any effect of striving for pathos, which is merely indicated by the presentation at the end of the section of Rachel weeping for her children in a speech of great power and restraint.

The last section, "The Flight into Egypt," presents Joseph and Mary being tempted by Voices of the Desert as they pursue their journey through the looking-glass, i.e. the journey of faith. These Voices seem to represent the temptations of the "normal" and particularly modern world;[8] they tempt with nonsense songs that sound like advertising commercials gone mad. (*The Age of Anxiety* employs this style extensively.) Joseph and Mary observe that insecurity is the condition natural to humanity: "Safe in Egypt we shall sigh/ For lost insecurity. . . ." Then follows a fine recitative interpreting the Flight as a redemption of the past: "Fly, Holy Family, from our immediate rage,/ That our future may be freed from our past. . . ." [9] The narrator's long speech modulating back to the present of Christmas trees and everyday life is both amusing and profound. The atmosphere of Christmas as it is for most of us is evoked with great precision, and contrasted with its religious meaning: "Once again/ As in previous years we have seen the actual Vision and failed/ To do more than entertain it as an agreeable/ Pos-

[8] Auden explains the symbolism of the Desert in *The Enchafèd Flood* (1950): it is the abode of those who reject or are rejected by the City, with the modern connotations of spiritual drouth, triviality, mechanization, and level uniformity. In "The Shield of Achilles" and "Plains" the Desert is the symbol of modern life at its worst.

[9] The manuscript of this is in the Lockwood Memorial Library at the University of Buffalo, in the *Sea and the Mirror* notebook.

sibility, once again we have sent Him away. . . ." We think of the future, of the coming of Lent and Good Friday; "But, for the time being, here we all are,/ Back in the moderate Aristotelian city," the everyday world. And to deal properly with this world and the present time is most difficult: "To those who have seen/ The Child, however dimly, however incredulously,/ The Time Being is, in a sense, the most trying time of all." To escape our guilt and inhibit our self-reflection, we are tempted to pray for temptation and suffering. They will come,[10] but "In the meantime/ There are bills to be paid, machines to keep in repair,/ Irregular verbs to learn, the Time Being to redeem/ From insignificance." In a metaphor developed later in "Nones" and in the rest of "Horae Canonicae," Auden says, "The happy morning is over,/ The night of agony still to come; the time is noon . . ."; and the soul knows that "God will cheat no one, not even the world of its triumph." [11] This magnificent conclusion is followed by a rather weak and anticlimactic chorus, perhaps necessary to carry out the musical analogy, but seeming flat on the page.

For the Time Being has enjoyed a good deal of popularity: as we have seen, an abridged version of it was set to music by Melvin Levy and performed in New York in 1959, and it is reprinted entire in *Modern Poetry,* edited by Maynard Mack, Leonard Dean, and William Frost (New York, 1950)—a widely used textbook—and in *Religious Drama 1,* edited by M. Halverson (New York, 1957); it is performed rather frequently by religious groups. Probably the fact that Eliot's *Four Quartets,* which embody many of the same themes (though in a very different way), happened to appear shortly before it has had much to do with the failure of the oratorio to impress the critics profoundly; comparison with Eliot's towering achievement is inevitable and the result is a foregone conclusion. The oratorio has also suffered from the equally inevitable comparison with the other work that originally appeared in the same volume with it, *The Sea and the Mirror,* which has seemed to most critics more brilliant, novel, and provocative, and therefore has the lion's share of their attention. Considered on its own terms, and at this distance in time, the work may be seen as a unique and remarkable success both formally and as a whole. The traditional forms of the Christmas pageant and oratorio are transformed and deepened to em-

[10] Cf. the epigraph: "Shall we continue in sin, that grace may abound? God forbid."
[11] In his review of translations of Kafka, *The New Republic,* 1941, Auden quotes Kafka's aphorism, "One must cheat no one, not even the world of its triumph." (It is included in the *Viking Book of Aphorisms,* p. 92.)

body the apprehension by the modern consciousness of the central event in history, understood psychologically, emotionally, and intellectually, by constant parallels with contemporary life; the various characters represent various types and also aspects of each of us, and the different episodes represent different aspects of the religious life of the individual, as well as the historical events. There is thus a great range and variety implicit in the scope of the piece, shown most obviously in the formal variety of verse and prose. Throughout, there is a triple consciousness at three levels: first, the unique historical event of the Incarnation; second, the collective, seasonal aspect of Christmas in its place in the Christian year, with its annual attempt to make it possible for Christ to be re-born, so to speak; and finally, the moment-to-moment effort of the individual to redeem everyday life from insignificance, to manifest the Incarnation in himself, to be a Christian. There are, as always in Auden, flaws and unevenness; but the central problem of rendering these three kinds of consciousness simultaneously is solved with brilliant success, and provides an adequate unifying principle for the enormous scope and variety of the piece. The oratorio does not seem dated or topical, nor does the religious attitude expressed seem in any way eccentric or extravagant. Auden placed the oratorio last both in *For the Time Being,* 1944, and in *Collected Poetry,* 1945, presumably because he felt, with justice, that it provided a very suitable conclusion for a volume.

Auden's Sacred Awe

by Richard M. Ohmann

By 1939 W. H. Auden, then thirty-two years old, was something of a monument. So magnetic was his name (and his presence) that a whole congeries of the most lustrous young poets—Day Lewis, MacNeice, Spender—had become known, somewhat ignominiously, as the "Auden group." Scarcely a young poet escaped his influence, and those who did, such as Dylan Thomas and George Barker, took shape on the literary scene as an *opposing* group, romantics in rebellion against an already established orthodoxy.

With Yeats dead and Eliot in early retirement (both of them political reactionaries, in any case), would-be king-makers looked to Auden as a likely successor, a poetic leader who might wave the anti-flags of his generation and create a new idiom for British verse. And why not? Auden had, indeed, brilliantly transmuted the modish talk of 1930 into a poetic style both familiar and strange. More to the point, perhaps, he had made pilgrimages to all the appropriate shrines of the intellectual left—Freud, Marx, Lawrence—taking from each a fashionable bit of inspiration. Whatever peculiarities the blend might seem to have, at least the ingredients were customary. All his credentials were in order, even to the symbolic tour of duty in Spain.

No wonder, then, that some threw eggs at the monument when, in the early stages of war with the common fascist enemy, Auden left England for America, began declaring that the artist had no stake in politics or causes, and (culminating betrayal) became a Christian. As Kierkegaard, Nietzsche, Tillich, Niebuhr, and other foreign gods appeared in his pantheon, there were disquieting readjustments in his thought.

Guilt, once the companion of sexual repression and social injustice, became for Auden an acknowledgment of original sin. The barely possi-

"Auden's Sacred Awe" by Richard M. Ohmann. From *The Commonweal,* LXXVIII (May 31, 1963), 279-81.

ble release from guilt was no longer Love, the personal and instinctual, but Love, the universal and redemptive. As an ideal, never attainable but always desirable, the Just City was replaced by Eden, a world without consequences.

When he put together his *Collected Poetry* in 1945, Auden deleted many poems, rewrote others, left out contexts, in a way that suggested to many critics an attempt to purge or digest the heresies of his youth. And meanwhile his style had lost its edge of tough obliqueness: it was still familiar, but not so simultaneously strange, not so contemptuous of grammatical subjects and articles. The critics complained: Auden had sold out. He had become trivial. He had substituted metaphysics for poetry. He had not written a good poem since the journey to Canterbury via America.

Oddly enough, when Auden was dropped by the enthusiasts of the radical thirties, no band of conservative, metaphysical critics stepped forth to adopt him. Less is written about him today, and with less passion, than twenty years ago. Few new poets, I would judge, consciously take Auden as a model, though Karl Shapiro is right in saying that Auden, more than any other poet, originally built the contemporary style. Perhaps the penalty for creating a landscape is that one becomes part of it, unnoticed.

Auden is an "established" poet, to be sure, solidly implanted in the anthologies and the modern poetry courses, winner of awards, called back to Oxford as Professor of Poetry. But the poems that sustain this reputation are, by and large, those of the thirties. The man is still with us, writing prolifically and well (although *Homage to Clio,* his latest volume of verse, is slight, *Nones* and *The Shield of Achilles* are full of superb poetry); yet for all public purposes Auden the poet is about as extinct as the trilobite, his continued real presence an embarrassment to critics, like that of the later Wordsworth, or of Eliot himself.

The demand for consistency in a poet is understandable: after all, the poet is part oracle and part priest, and in these *personae* gross vacillation can be unseemly. But surely it is time to agree that in so far as we have embalmed Auden on the grounds of heart failure and ruptured technique, we have botched our diagnosis, whatever the theory behind our treatment.

Look at Auden's works from a reasonable distance, and the consistencies are more striking than the shifts—certainly as obvious as those which make one corpus of Donne's work, or Dryden's, or Yeats'. Particularly valuable in providing distance is the newly published [1962] collection of Auden's criticism, *The Dyer's Hand* (Random House. $7.50). Here are assembled fifteen years' worth of major comments on literature, which serves as a gloss on his early poetry no less than on his later.

Before condemning Auden for shifts in allegiance, it is sensible to reconsider the relationship between art and belief, a matter on which Auden himself is quite articulate. Poetry, he says, has in it a strong element of *play*—the formal characteristics emphasize pure disinterested sound, not message. It is ill-suited to controversy, therefore, and should have no ulterior purpose except, "by telling the truth, to disenchant and disintoxicate." It should simply dwell mnemonically on things as they are.

Ideas are less important for the poet than the way in which they are entertained, less important than their emotional accompaniment. As Auden has it, "in poetry, all facts and all beliefs cease to be true or false and become interesting possibilities," though the poet must be emotionally *involved* in them as a man.

Now this is not the only position that can be defended, but it is a respectable one. To criticize Auden for setting emotion above ideology and causes is no more reasonable than to attack Swift for preferring sanity and good will to "projects," or Voltaire for making Candide retreat from philosophy to the garden, or Arnold for rejecting the "machinery" of social reform in favor of culture.

Nor, I think, is it even possible to see in Auden's verse, as Randall Jarrell did twenty years ago, a retreat from definite programs, a failure of the impulse to action. As early as his undergraduate years, Auden had told Spender that the poet must have "no decided views which he seeks to put across in his poetry." And looking back now at his poems of the thirties, one can see only with difficulty how readers in those days could have taken them for expressions of political doctrine.

True, Auden could roar at the newspaper magnate,

> Beethameer, Beethameer, bully of Britain,
> With your face as fat as a farmer's bum;
> . . . you'll get the thrashing you richly deserve

but his clinical irony undermined the revolutionary excess of the speaker as surely as his invective destroyed the capitalist.

There is in this early poetry no sentimentalizing of the masses: the six beggared cripples who long "to dine with Lord Lobcock and Count Asthma on the platinum benches" are as foolish in their values as the rich they envy. Society is sick, top to bottom. Moreover, Auden was from the start too complex an intellectual to find peace in panaceas; he could never state one position without feeling the tug of its opposite, and his interest in leftist reform movements scarcely went beyond their psychological impact on society.

So it should be no surprise to find Auden saying now, as he has been saying at least since 1940, that poets are ill-equipped to traffic in politics, since their main concern is with the individual and with emotional relationships. What kind of climate does society offer for the flourishing of art, and of the self?—this is the only "political" question that remains alive for Auden. Thus he laments the rise of our bland, anonymous public, the decline of folk art, the absence of a sense of community among artists, and, especially, the loss of a sense that the public realm is a "sphere of revelatory personal deeds." The machine and the state have slain the hero, robbed poetry of its traditional human subject, substituted "behavior" for deeds.

In response to mass society, however, Auden offers, not a political ideology, but the idea of the community, bound by love; not Utopia, but Eden (an absolute monarchy, by the way, with pageantry, play, and Victorian furniture, and with no cars, movies, planes, television sets or radios). In short, Auden is simply not competing in the political marketplace. But neither did he do so in the thirties: those revolutionaries in his poems who set off over mountains in lonely exile were not looking for a Marxist paradise, but for "new styles of architecture, a change of heart," a recovery of psychic health in themselves and in society.

Auden's apoliticalism can lead him to insensitivity when he does discuss social issues. He claims, for instance, that the whole question of Communism, socialism, and capitalism is merely a "party issue," a debate over practical means to an agreed-upon end, not a revolutionary issue which turns on differences in principle.

This is, of course, preposterous. To ignore the heartbreaking human consequences of unregenerate capitalism (i.e., *pure* capitalism) or of totalitarian Communism is to lose touch with feeling, as well as with social thought. But as poet and critic, Auden need not play the political theorist. And indeed, in these critical essays his notion of society is more a source of metaphors than a program.

The "city," one of his preoccupations, is a state of mind and a way of organizing moral experience, and has geographical existence only on the map of the emotions—like Belmont and Venice in Auden's treatment of *The Merchant of Venice*. Or, more typically still, he speaks of works of art themselves as cities, as verbal societies, possessing at best an order not attainable in the fallen real world. What then is the political function of art? Only to remind the politicians that those they govern "are people with faces, not anonymous members."

If Auden, as poet and critic, is nearly apolitical, his religious beliefs, too, reside mainly beneath the artistic surface, as little more than "interesting possibilities." Long ago he argued that although all important art contains buried metaphysics, the writer is unwise to insist on his metaphysics overtly.

About the only dogmas he holds crucial to the artist are these three: a historical world exists, and its existence is good; that world is nonetheless fallen; that world is redeemable. Nor does one often find in his poetry a less ambiguous statement of belief than this:

> For the end, for me as for cities,
> Is total absence: what comes to be
> Must go back into non-being
> For the sake of the equity, the rhythm
> Past measure or comprehending.

Lines of the fifties, but who could tell that a conversion lies between them and these of the thirties?

> And Tomorrow
> Comes. It's a world. It's a way.

The speaking voice of Auden's verse rarely claims to know the answers, whatever Auden the man may know.

His concern, then, is not with ideas as true or false, but with ideas as felt, and still more pronouncedly, with feelings themselves, intellectualized, ordered, and generalized. The poet's business is to start with "a crowd of recollected occasions of feeling," and transform the crowd into a community. Auden is our theologian of the emotions, our geographer of the self.

The Dyer's Hand shows him scrutinizing moral and emotional experience, setting up a calculus of desire, guilt, repentance, love, boredom, and the rest, dissecting the psyche and its images of itself, just as in his poetry he has always collapsed incident, shining object, and countryside into structures of feeling. It is not really very far from his early "Paysage Moralisé" to his later "Bucolics," which, though they give us somewhat more of the visual and concrete, still have their artistic center in psychology.

Yet for all this preoccupation with emotion, Auden is the most impersonal of poets: "unless the poet sacrifices his feelings completely to the poem," the poem fails. And not just *his* feelings, but all particularity of feeling, for Auden's dedication is to the type, not the individual. Our sufferings are only poetically interesting, he contends, in so far as they are typical of the human condition, and for "sufferings" he might have substituted the name of any emotion: Auden dearly loves a generalization.

This bent altogether dominates his criticism, which bulges with dichotomies, categories, and distinctions, to the extent that he seems more interested in extraliterary insights exampled by the works than in the works themselves. Thus his discussion of *Othello* proceeds out of a distinction between the villain and the criminal, his treatment of Ibsen and Cervantes out of a distinction between the hero as genius and the hero as apostle, his essay on Frost out of a distinction between poems dominated by truth (Prospero poems—Frost is Prospero-dominated) and poems dominated by beauty (Ariel poems). Eden and the New Jerusalem, the I and the Ego, deeds and behavior: the book moves through a whirl of divisions and categories, in which the unique detail virtually disappears behind its significance.

In his poetry, too, detail quickly yields to meaning. It is interesting to remember how many of his poems view landscapes from mountain passes, cliffs, planes—how enamored he is of the "spell of high places"; from such points of vantage no leaf or stone is visible, but only pattern. In general, Auden steps back from the swarm of things so as to piece out the pattern, and his vantage point is psychological and moral.

Compare two ways of looking at a wood, one Frost's, one Auden's:

> The hard snow held me, save where now and then
> One foot went through. The view was all in lines
> Straight up and down of tall slim trees
> Too much alike to mark or name a place by . . .
>
> [—Frost, "The Wood-Pile"]

Guilty intention still looks for a hotel
That wants no details and surrenders none;
A wood is that, and throws in charm as well,
And many a semi-innocent, undone,
Has blamed its nightingales who round the deed
Sang with such sweetness of a happy greed.
[—Auden, "Woods"]

There are shadows of significance behind Frost's trees, to be sure: in his wood a man will understand how capable nature is of a frightening, inhuman blankness. Yet the parallel trees and the crusty snow are at least as much there as the emotions they prompt. Frost cares about *seeing* the wood. Auden's stanza begins with guilty intention and ends with happy greed, and the wood itself, though it occasions the speculations, makes only a courtesy appearance. Its trees are neither straight nor twisted. It is not this wood, that wood, or any wood, but an archetype, a total abstraction from experience. The real world is for Auden an allegorical text, and the intellectual constructs that can be placed upon it are paramount.

The danger of this method is obvious: the poet may end by dispensing with life; his poems may transform the unique into "An algebraic formula,/ An abstract model of events," as he put it once. Yet Auden's work is remarkably alive. What keeps it from mummifying experience? *The Dyer's Hand,* I think, points to an answer.

In these essays, Auden insists on the poet's feeling of "sacred awe" before some objects, beings, and events. There are parts of the world which inexplicably ignite his imagination, and before which he does homage in verse. The awe and reverence are there in Auden's own poetry. They are the force which mediates between detail and schema, particular and general, object and thought. It is sacred awe, a sense of the power and meaning that permeates experience, which animates the abstractions of this highly intellectual poet, and which should preserve him, finally, from the charge of ideological fickleness. For he is a celebrant of things, not a partisan.

Chronology of Important Dates

1907	Wystan Hugh Auden born in York. Moved to Birmingham, 1908.
1915-20	St. Edmund's School (preparatory). Began friendship with Christopher Isherwood.
1920-25	Gresham's School, Holt; specialized in biology. First poem published, 1924.
1925-28	Christ Church College, Oxford. *Poems* privately printed by Stephen Spender, 1928.
1928-29	Berlin.
1930-35	Schoolmaster at Larchfield Academy, Helensburgh, Scotland, and at The Downs School, Colwall, near Malvern. *Poems,* 1930, containing "Paid on Both Sides: A Charade" and 30 poems; second edition, 1933. *The Orators,* 1932. *The Dance of Death,* 1933.
1935	Collaborated with Christopher Isherwood on play, *The Dog Beneath the Skin.* Worked for six months with G.P.O. Film Unit, collaborating with Benjamin Britten on *Coal-Face, Night Mail,* and other films. Edited, with John Garrett, *The Poet's Tongue,* an anthology.
1936	Trip to Iceland with Louis MacNeice; their joint *Letters from Iceland* published, 1937. Another play, *The Ascent of F6,* written with Isherwood. *Look, Stranger!* published. (The American edition, whose title—*On This Island*—Auden preferred, appeared in 1937.)
1937	Trip to Spain during Civil War. The poem *Spain* published.
1938	Trip to China with Christopher Isherwood; their *Journey to a War* published, 1939. *On the Frontier,* another play, written with Isherwood. Edited *Oxford Book of Light Verse.*
1939	Permanent move to United States in January, with Isherwood. Became U.S. Citizen, 1946. Taught at St. Mark's School, Mass., and the New School for Social Research, N.Y.
1940	*Another Time* published.
1941-42	Taught at University of Michigan. Collaborated with Benjamin Britten on *Paul Bunyan,* a choral operetta, 1941. *The Double Man* published, 1941 (English title: *New Year Letter*).

1942-45	Taught at Swarthmore College. Taught concurrently at Bryn Mawr, 1943-45. *For the Time Being* published, 1944. Edited *A Selection of the Poems of Alfred Lord Tennyson,* 1944.
1945	*Collected Poetry* published.
1946-47	Taught at Bennington and Barnard Colleges and at New School. *The Age of Anxiety* published, 1947. Editor of "Yale Series of Younger Poets," 1947-57.
1948	Awarded Pultizer Prize. Edited *The Portable Greek Reader.*
1950	*Collected Shorter Poems, 1930-1944,* published in London. *The Enchafèd Flood: or The Romantic Iconography of the Sea* published. Edited, with Norman Holmes Pearson, *Poets of the English Language* (5 vols.).
1951	*The Rake's Progress,* by Igor Stravinsky, with libretto by Auden and Chester Kallman, performed. *Nones* published. 1951-58, with Lionel Trilling and Jacques Barzun, served as critic for Reader's Subscription Book Club, and 1959-62, for The Mid-Century Book Club.
1954	Awarded Bollingen Prize for 1953. Elected to American Academy of Arts and Letters.
1955	*The Shield of Achilles* published. Received National Book Award, 1956.
1956-61	Professor of Poetry, Oxford University.
1956	English version (with Chester Kallman) of *The Magic Flute* for the Mozart bicentenary performed on NBC-TV and published. *The Old Man's Road* published. Edited *Selected Writings of Sydney Smith, The Faber Book of Modern American Verse.*
1958	*Selected Poetry* published.
1960	*Homage to Clio* published.
1961	Libretto (with Chester Kallman) for *Elegy for Young Lovers,* by Hans Werner Henze, performed and published. English version (with Kallman) of Mozart's *Don Giovanni* performed on NBC-TV and published.
1962	*The Dyer's Hand* (new and selected criticism) published. Translated (with Elizabeth Mayer) Goethe's *Italian Journey.* Edited (with Louis Kronenberger) *The Viking Book of Aphorisms.*

Notes on the Editor and Authors

MONROE K. SPEARS, editor of the anthology, is professor of English at Rice University. He was editor of *The Sewanee Review* from 1952 to 1961, and is the author of *The Poetry of W. H. Auden: The Disenchanted Island* (1963).

JOHN BAYLEY is Fellow and Tutor in English of New College, Oxford. His latest book is *Characters of Love: A Study in the Literature of Personality* (1960).

CLEANTH BROOKS, well-known critic, teaches at Yale. His most recent book is *William Faulkner: The Yoknapatawpha Country* (1964).

EDWARD CALLAN teaches at Western Michigan University in Kalamazoo.

G. S. FRASER, British critic, was in the United States as Visiting Professor 1963-64 at the University of Rochester. In addition to *Vision and Rhetoric* (1959), he is the author of *The Modern Writer and His World* (1953).

RICHARD HOGGART, Professor of English at the University of Birmingham, England, has written, aside from his work on Auden, *The Uses of Literacy* (1957).

CHRISTOPHER ISHERWOOD lives in Santa Monica, Calif. His latest novel is *Down There on a Visit* (1962).

CARLO IZZO, Professor of English at the University of Bologna, Italy, has written histories of both English and American literature and has edited, and translated into Italian, anthologies of contemporary American and English poetry. Auden's "Goodbye to the Mezzogiorno," in *Homage to Clio,* is dedicated to him.

FREDERICK P. W. MCDOWELL is Professor of English at the University of Iowa and author of *Elizabeth Madox Roberts* (1963).

MARIANNE MOORE, one of America's most distinguished poets, lives in Brooklyn.

RICHARD OHMANN teaches at Wesleyan University in Connecticut. He is the author of *Shaw: the Style and the Man* (1962).

STEPHEN SPENDER, poet and critic, edits the magazine *Encounter;* his most recent book is *The Struggle of the Modern* (1963).

EDMUND WILSON, well-known critic and man of letters, lives in Oneida County, New York.

Selected Bibliography

There are four books devoted exclusively to Auden. Francis Scarfe, *W. H. Auden* (Monaco: The Lyrebird Press, 1949) is a brief (69 pages) survey. Richard Hoggart, *Auden: An Introductory Essay* (London: Chatto and Windus, 1951) is the first full-scale treatment, and the same author's *W. H. Auden* (London: Longmans, Green & Company, Ltd., 1957: Writers and Their Work, No. 93) in the British Council series is an attractive introduction. Joseph Warren Beach, *The Making of the Auden Canon* (Minneapolis: University of Minnesota Press, 1957), is "meant to be a record of the facts in regard to W. H. Auden's procedure in making up the texts of the *Collected Poetry* (Random House, 1945) and the *Collected Shorter Poems* (Faber & Faber, Ltd., 1950) . . ." (p. 3). Monroe K. Spears, *The Poetry of W. H. Auden: The Disenchanted Island* (New York and London: Oxford University Press, 1963), is the most comprehensive study to date; it includes a chronology, a bibliography of Auden's writings, and a first-line index giving the publication history of each poem. A full-scale bibliography of Auden's writings through 1955, by B. C. Bloomfield, has been announced by the University of Virginia Press for publication in 1964.

The following list is a selection from the numerous articles and parts of books dealing with Auden:

Bogan, Louise. "The Quest of W. H. Auden," in *Selected Criticism* (New York: Noonday Press, 1955).

Brooks, Cleanth. "W. H. Auden as a Critic," *The Kenyon Review,* XXVI (Winter, 1964), 173-89.

Callan, Edward. "An Annotated Checklist of the Works of W. H. Auden," *Twentieth Century Literature,* IV (April-July, 1958), 30-50. (Also published as a book: Denver: Alan Swallow, Publisher.)

————. "The Development of W. H. Auden's Poetic Theory Since 1940," *Twentieth Century Literature,* IV (October, 1958), 79-91.

Clancy, Joseph P. "A. W. H. Auden Bibliography, 1924-1955," *Thought,* XXX (Summer, 1955), 260-70.

Cox, R. G. "The Poetry of W. H. Auden," in *The Modern Age,* Vol. VII of "The Pelican Guide to English Literature," Boris Ford, ed. (Baltimore: Penguin Books, Inc., 1961), pp. 377-93.

Day Lewis, Cecil. *The Buried Day* (New York: Harper & Row, Publishers, 1960). Autobiographical.

Grigson, Geoffrey, ed. *New Verse,* "Auden Double Number" (Nov., 1937).

Isherwood, Christopher. *Lions and Shadows: An Education in the Twenties* (London: Hogarth Press, 1937). Autobiographical.

Jarrell, Randall. "Changes of Attitude and Rhetoric in Auden's Poetry," *The Southern Review,* VII (Autumn, 1941), 326-49.

———. "Freud to Paul: The Stages of Auden's Ideology," *Partisan Review,* XII (Fall, 1945), 437-57.

MacNeice, Louis. *Modern Poetry: A Personal Essay* (London: Oxford University Press, 1938).

Ostroff, Anthony, ed. A symposium on Auden's "A Change of Air," with essays by George P. Elliott, Karl Shapiro, and Stephen Spender, and a reply by W. H. Auden. *The Kenyon Review,* XXVI (Winter, 1964), 190-208.

Rosenthal, Moritz. *The Modern Poets: An Introduction* (New York: Oxford University Press, Inc., 1955).

Roth, R. M. "The Sophistication of W. H. Auden: A Sketch in Longinian Method," *Modern Philology,* XLVIII (Feb., 1951), 193-204.

Spears, Monroe K. "Late Auden: The Satirist as Lunatic Clergyman," *The Sewanee Review,* LIX (Winter, 1951), 50-74.

———. "The Dominant Symbols of Auden's Poetry," *The Sewanee Review,* LIX (Summer, 1951), 392-425.

Spender, Stephen. *World Within World* (London: Hamish Hamilton, 1951). Autobiographical.

TWENTIETH CENTURY VIEWS

British Authors

JANE AUSTEN, edited by Ian Watt (S-TC-26)
THE BEOWULF POET, edited by Donald K. Fry (S-TC-82)
BLAKE, edited by Northrop Frye (S-TC-58)
BYRON, edited by Paul West (S-TC-31)
COLERIDGE, edited by Kathleen Coburn (S-TC-70)
CONRAD, edited by Marvin Mudrick S-TC-53)
DICKENS, edited by Martin Price (S-TC-72)
JOHN DONNE, edited by Helen Gardner (S-TC-19)
DRYDEN, edited by Bernard N. Schilling (S-TC-32)
T. S. ELIOT, edited by Hugh Kenner (S-TC-2)
FIELDING, edited by Ronald Paulson (S-TC-9)
FORSTER, edited by Malcolm Bradbury (S-TC-59)
HARDY, edited by Albert Guérard (S-TC-25)
HOPKINS, edited by Geoffrey H. Hartman (S-TC-57)
A. E. HOUSMAN, edited by Christopher Ricks (S-TC-83)
SAMUEL JOHNSON, edited by Donald J. Greene (S-TC-48)
BEN JONSON, edited by Jonas A. Barish (S-TC-22)
KEATS, edited by Walter Jackson Bate (S-TC-43)
D. H. LAWRENCE, edited by Mark Spilka (S-TC-24)
MARLOWE, edited by Clifford Leech (S-TC-44)
ANDREW MARVELL, edited by George deF. Lord (S-TC-81)
MILTON, edited by Louis L. Martz (S-TC-60)
MODERN BRITISH DRAMATISTS, edited by John Russell Brown (S-TC-74)
OSCAR WILDE, edited by Richard Ellmann (S-TC-87)
RESTORATION DRAMATISTS, edited by Earl Miner (S-TC-64)
SAMUEL RICHARDSON, edited by John Carroll (S-TC-85)
SHAKESPEARE: THE COMEDIES, edited by Kenneth Muir (S-TC-47)
SHAKESPEARE: THE HISTORIES, edited by Eugene M. Waith (S-TC-45)
SHAKESPEARE: THE TRAGEDIES, edited by Alfred Harbage (S-TC-40)
G. B. SHAW, edited by R. J. Kaufmann (S-TC-50)
SHELLEY, edited by George M. Ridenour (S-TC-49)
SPENSER, edited by Harry Berger, Jr. (S-TC-80)
LAURENCE STERNE, edited by John Traugott (S-TC-77)
SWIFT, edited by Ernest Tuveson (S-TC-35)
THACKERAY, edited by Alexander Welsh (S-TC-75)
DYLAN THOMAS, edited by Charles B. Cox (S-TC-56)
YEATS, edited by John Unterecker (S-TC-23)

TWENTIETH CENTURY VIEWS

American Authors

AUDEN, edited by Monroe K. Spears (S-TC-38)
STEPHEN CRANE, edited by Maurice Bassan (S-TC-66)
EMILY DICKINSON, edited by Richard B. Sewall (S-TC-28)
EMERSON, edited by Milton R. Konvitz
and Stephen E. Whicher (S-TC-12)
FAULKNER, edited by Robert Penn Warren (S-TC-65)
F. SCOTT FITZGERALD, edited by Arthur Mizener (S-TC-27)
ROBERT FROST, edited by James M. Cox (S-TC-3)
HAWTHORNE, edited by A. N. Kaul (S-TC-55)
HEMINGWAY, edited by Robert P. Weeks (S-TC-8)
HENRY JAMES, edited by Leon Edel (S-TC-34)
SINCLAIR LEWIS, edited by Mark Schorer (S-TC-6)
ROBERT LOWELL, edited by Thomas Parkinson (S-TC-79)
MELVILLE, edited by Richard Chase (S-TC-13)
ARTHUR MILLER, edited by Robert W. Corrigan (S-TC-84)
MODERN AMERICAN DRAMATISTS, edited by Alvin B. Kernan (S-TC-69)
O'NEILL, edited by John Gassner (S-TC-39)
POE, edited by Robert Regan (S-TC-63)
EZRA POUND, edited by Walter Sutton (S-TC-29)
WALLACE STEVENS, edited by Marie Borroff (S-TC-33)
THOREAU, edited by Sherman Paul (S-TC-10)
MARK TWAIN, edited by Henry Nash Smith (S-TC-30)
EDITH WHARTON, edited by Irving Howe (S-TC-20)
WHITMAN, edited by Roy Harvey Pearce (S-TC-5)
W. C. WILLIAMS, edited by J. Hillis Miller (S-TC-61)